Wm. L. D

Dec 1936

# RELIGION AND CULTURE SERIES

*Joseph Husslein, S.J., Ph.D., General Editor*

# A Preface to Life

# A Preface to Life

## Is Life Worth Living?

By

**FATHER JAMES, O.M.Cap.**

M.A., Ph.D., D.Litt., Agrégé en Philosophie
à l'Université Catholique de Louvain

THE BRUCE PUBLISHING COMPANY
MILWAUKEE

Imprimi potest:

FR. EDWIN, O.M.CAP.,
Min. Prov. Hib.

Nihil obstat:

H. E. RIES,
Censor librorum

Imprimatur:

✠ SAMUEL A. STRITCH,
Archiepiscopus Milwaukiensis

April 27, 1936

To

S. M. A.

# Preface by the General Editor

A quick succession of distinctive volumes, dealing with religious and philosophic themes, has issued from the pen of Father James in recent years. Of these the present book is the first to go forth under American auspices. Yet the series of which it constitutes a part is itself international in purpose and scope, as the Catholic Revival which it strives to promote.

Father James, O.M.Cap., known also under his secular name of E. O'Mahony, President of St. Bonaventure's University Hostel at Cork, is no mere philosopher of the schools. His interests, as this volume testifies, are with the men and women in office and shop, and with the people everywhere in the great world at large. His object is to give them an intelligent introduction to that true and sound philosophy of life which is the special need of our day. He has therefore called his volume A PREFACE TO LIFE.

In the prime of his powers, Father James has been eager to deal out, with both hands at once, the largess of his study, of his thought and observation. Yet every page here offered is indicative of accuracy and care, of sureness of touch and mastery of style which not seldom rises to beauty and eloquence of diction. There is keenness of observation and originality of conception in his matter and presentation.

Yet it would be false to say that here is a book "to read as one runs." It is not so simple. In fact, no winged Pegasus has yet been discovered in the realm of Philosophy. We must do our own climbing, with a trusty guide at our side, if we would reach the coveted summit. But there are glorious outlooks as we scale the heights that can make us quite forget our toil. And there are pleasant places where the grass is green and the waters gurgle in the spring, and all about us the air is pure, while far above the light rests fair and golden on the towering cliffs.

One thing the reader will quickly discover in this volume. It is that every man is instinctively at least a philosopher, no matter through what colored glasses he may view the world. Since this is so, the one important thing must evidently be to provide that his philosophy is true, that it leads him onward toward a fuller light and wider vision, that it combines with faith, so that, as on two strong wings, his spirit may soar to the font and well of Truth Eternal. To aid in this sublime attainment is the author's highest purpose.

JOSEPH HUSSLEIN, S.J., PH.D.
*General Editor, Religion and Culture Series*

St. Louis University,
May 17, 1936.

# Author's Preface

Alternative titles for the book that is now about to leave my hands were embarrassingly numerous and for a time I dallied with the thought of calling it simply *A Philosophy of Life*. This temptation was quickly overcome when behind the mask of apparent modesty I discerned the real ambitions of such an undertaking. A philosophy of life, as I view it, ought to provide a large practical wisdom begotten of a rich and long experience: it should be in a position to suggest a sure and settled outlook on the very many things that go to make up what men call life.

Experience, I am sure, is not merely what happens to a man, it is not an affair of gray hairs only, or of many years, or of varied contacts with life. It is a man's reactions to life's happenings that constitute his experience and for that the important thing is a man's own vision, his capacity for being spiritually alive and intuitively alert, his power of seeing and hearing significant things and of making use of them. But there is inevitably action and reaction in this matter. While youth may see visions, it is for age to judge the sincerity of its own youthful enthusiasms. Many a man has been a hero in his dreams who in actual life was surprised and shocked at his own knavery. The test of youth's philosophy is its capacity to survive a young man's contact with the world, and one needs to be very old, I should think, before one can dare to assess the value of one's own philosophy in all its details or offer to the public what may be called even *a* philosophy of life.

It is possible, however, without fear of the future to suggest, as it were by way of a preface to life, what such a philosophy must be. It is this more modest task that I have set myself in the pages which follow. The title, finally selected, has, therefore, the advantage of covering what I desire to say, while the added subtitle, associated with the name of Mallock, indicates not merely the philosophic trend of the book, but is a query calculated to arouse the curiosity of the public for whom it is intended.

FR. JAMES, O.M.Cap.

St. Bonaventure's University Hostel,
Cork, Ireland

# Contents

# A Preface to Life

# Introduction

In this book I am embarking on the perilous adventure of writing an essay in popular philosophy. The topic broached therein is one that might well engage the attention of a technical philosopher; it is nothing short of an attempt to lay the foundations of a complete philosophy of life. But the manner of its discussion, it is hoped, will be such as to appeal to the average man. I have chiefly before my mind those people who are shy of philosophy as one might be of a long-neglected friend, or simply because in their minds philosophy is associated with aristocracy and leisured luxury.

It is not easy to avoid being acutely conscious of the danger that lies in this attempt to hold up to life the mirror of philosophy. The description of one's findings may irritate philosophers proper and command only faint praise from the average man. But a little experience in introducing young men of the Church and the University, as well as those true aristocrats who call themselves plain men of the city, to philosophy has emboldened me to undertake the task. Philosophy seemed to come to them, hallowed though it is, in pleasant guise, awakening them to the wonder of existence and the unsuspected glory of human life. Philosophy, they felt, pointed constantly beyond itself, and a moment came when expectantly human reason awaited a new light on life. As with Dante, the hour struck when Virgil ceased to guide:

> What reason here discovers, I have power
> To show thee: that which lies beyond, expect
> From Beatrice, faith not reason's task.[1]

The light of "what lies beyond" is the vision that Christians possess for the present by faith, and in their contact with philosophy, I have found, a new sense of religion and of its place in life came to those who cultivated it. Philosophy is greatest when in its self-abasement it recognizes what goes beyond it, and certainly the last word of pure philosophy is to recognize the Mystery of Him who planned the universe. A God that philosophy, the instrument of a finite mind, could comprehend would be no God. But a God who could not, if He so willed, reveal His Mind and give to the human intellect a deeper vision of reality and of Himself would not be less unacceptable to human reason. Pure philosophy leads us, then, to the very threshold of the supernatural; it impinges on a region which many suppose lies entirely beyond its sphere. But as long as the horizon of the human mind is the wide firmament of all reality, of being whose nature is to be without limit, the human intellect is open for the light of faith which is the beginning of an eternal vision. In this new light the human mind does not cease to be itself; it

---

[1] *Purg.,* xviii, 47–48.

is never more itself, in fact, than when it avows its incompetency to solve all its problems, and accepts the added light that comes to it in faith. Both reason and faith have one Orient, the Eternal Light that enlighteneth every man that comes into the world.

If reason under the illumination of Faith does not cease to be itself, it must defend itself against attacks. For that defense it must be equipped with the weapons of philosophy. The war that is waged on religion today is inspired by false ideas and sophistry. Everywhere the battle is waged, in the press, in books, on the streets. Too often even educated Catholics are shaken by the first impact of erroneous theories: they quickly seek the ramparts of their Faith. But no man can for long live a twofold life, or make intellectual cowardice the condition of his Faith. There is no problem, begotten of human minds, that can shake the Christian's sanity; there is no reasoning, even of the greatest minds, which can convince him of the absurdity of his Faith. But to unmask the sophisms of the adversary he must be intellectually equipped and know what the normal Christian is expected to know concerning the rational grounds upon which his Faith reposes; false philosophy must be vanquished by true philosophy.

It is not enough, however, to be always on the defensive. The Christian must strive to think out his Faith, to see its far-reaching implications. Faith was not intended merely to illuminate the mind alone: it must flow into life and determine the Christian's judgments of the things that count. For this purpose philosophy must serve to articulate our faith, to expand its intrinsic light, to fling its rays into all departments of our lives. A philosophy that is inspired by faith can bring religion out of the secret sanctuary of the heart and confront it with the problems of the day, problems of the State and Society, problems of economic and political significance, to command human judgments on them that are Christian. It were little use to combat the laicization and secularization of society which Pope Pius XI has designated the heresy of our age until we have got to the root of the matter in the human spirit. External civilization is only an outward expression of inner mind, and until we have Christianized our minds by true philosophy there is little hope of a Christian civilization.

St. Thomas of Aquin has been called the first of modern philosophers because he distinguished between reason and faith and found an autonomous basis for philosophy as the outcome of unaided reason. But St. Thomas would be the last to claim that philosophy was autonomous or self-sufficient under all its aspects. Philosophy, he held, gave rise to problems that reason could not finally solve; the human mind even in the zenith of philosophic effort was still "open" for a new perfection of its powers that comes in supernatural faith and ultimately in divine vision. His own mind was strengthened by the power of faith, and it is useless to seek out psychologically where his faith began as his human reason reached the limits of its powers. To discover that would be just as impossible as to find in the psychological life of the ordinary man where his senses end and intelligence begins, or to isolate a pure sensation in the organic process of knowledge where the senses and intelligence are acting at one and the same time. The fact is that the mind of Aquinas was enlightened by his faith, and in practice he did not *separate* philosophy from theology though he very clearly *distinguished* the domains of reason and faith.

The secularization or laicization of which the present Holy Father, Pope Pius XI, has so luminously written in regard to social and civic life is something ingrained in the outlook of even Christian thinkers. A separatist philosophy is as much a symptom of it as a laicized civilization where religion is divorced from social life. At the moment of writing philosophers are much engaged with solving the problem of whether there can be such a thing as Christian Philosophy at all or not. It would be out of place to enter into a discussion of that problem here. No amount of analysis or discussion can get rid of the fact that there is, and has been, a Christian Philosophy of life. That the Thomistic *distinction* of reason and faith, of philosophy and theology, useful when it was a question of meeting adversaries who said our philosophy was theology and indistinguishable from faith, should have grown into a *separation* of the two disciplines of a Christian mind is, I make bold to think, deplorable. I cannot do better than conclude with Pius XI's own words, which must give new hope to those of us who do insist that there is a Christian Philosophy and that Christian Philosophy is the only redemption for our epoch.[2] The occasion was when the Holy Father addressed a group of five hundred University students in Rome. After congratulating them on their interest in Catholic Philosophy, and complimenting them for not doubting, not even by a query, the existence of such a thing as Christian Philosophy, he goes

---

[2]My views on this matter of Christian Philosophy will be found in my various books, particularly in *Life and Religion*, and in two lectures in *Moral Principles and Practice* (Cambridge Lectures).

on to say: "Christianity is in fact a vision of life and of the world, a *Weltanschauung* as the Germans call it, and the textbook of this vision, its twofold manual, is to be found in the two *Summas* of St. Thomas."[3] The book which follows is inspired by this philosophy of St. Thomas, and is intended to suggest the broad outlines of a Christian Philosophy of life.

---

[3]*Observatore Romano*, 16, IX, 1933.

# 1

# Philosophy and the Plain Man

The word *philosophy* tends to awe the plain man. It comes to him hoary with associations of aristocracy. Intellectual magnates, like Plato and Aristotle, are not likely to inspire confidence in one whose job in life is not thought or speculative inquiry. Little wonder if he is inclined to let philosophy go by, for "the poor make no new friends."

The average man need have no such misgivings. Philosophy, the thing, is much more homely than the word. "Homely" does not convey the true idea either, unless it signifies that philosophy is as much at home with the average man as it is with the aristocrat. There is a moment in the life of every individual when the philosopher in him awakens.

That moment strikes when for the first time a young man feels the need of answering for himself the questions that he was satisfied to put to others in his childhood. The conceit of opinion that comes with adolescence, the feeling of isolated responsibility, the desire to live one's own life, are things that bring with them a call to construct some kind of system, a philosophy of the universe. In this new vocation things thoughtlessly learned in childhood begin to assume significance, literature is cultivated for its vision and noble feelings, but above all the young man feels that he must begin to look out upon the world and upon the panorama of his life that stretches dimly out before him, no longer through the eyes of others, but through his own, in order to see things for himself.

Did he only know it, such an individual is experiencing the awakening of the philosopher in him. If practical life, and urgent necessities of existence, do not crowd too fully or too insistently in upon him, sooner or later he will have achieved something like a philosophy. Man is a link in the great chain of life. Above him are beings endowed with intelligence that does not need an organism of senses; below him are those beings possessed of senses but lacking mind. In man there is a marriage of sense and intellect. Of this marriage was begotten philosophy as we know it. By means of his senses a man is brought into contact with a vast material world around him. This contact acts as a spur to thought, and when he tries to look out on the universe through his own eyes, a man is definitely faced with the task of interpretation. The world hands out its problems to him, and within him he feels the instinctive stirrings of his mind to solve them. The desire to know is natural.

That this desire does not burn brightly in the sanctuary of every human mind is no proof of its non-reality. Many are so hemmed in by daily occupations that they are scarcely conscious of their own desires. But let nature express itself, develop naturally, and from the little child to the old philosopher you will see the human mind actively in search of knowledge. Knowledge is the food of mind, its true aliment, and it hungers for it as bodies do for bread.

That great philosopher, Aquinas, who somehow in these days has become the friend of all men, was constantly emphasizing that the desire to know sprang from the very soil of human nature. From his Commentary on Aristotle we may select two of the fundamental reasons urged by him which seem to us of singular importance. Everyone will admit that things are naturally impelled to their own characteristic activities. It is as natural for bodies to fall through space as it is for the sun to shine or flowers to blossom. Ways and means of preventing these activities can be devised, of course. But that naturally, when left to themselves, they will show themselves in typical modes of action and behavior is not thereby obscured or denied. It is exactly the same with man's desire to know. For it is precisely by thought that man is distinct from all other beings and occupies his place in the scheme of things. It follows that knowledge which is the result of a man's thinking will be something for which his nature craves.

The second reason assigned by St. Thomas is still more interesting and of broader significance. Everything, he argues, desires its own proper perfection and development. But it is by virtue of his possession of intelligence that man is what he is. As found in man, however, intellect in its initial stages is imperfect. It needs to be fecundated by contact with reality before it can beget its ideas which result for it in knowledge. The imperfect human intellect advances in perfection, it grows and develops, according as it grows in knowledge. There is accordingly in the human mind that general tendency of imperfect things which seeks and demands its proper perfection, knowledge. The desire to know is natural.

In developing this proof of the natural character of man's desire to know, St. Thomas culls from Aristotle a phrase of extreme significance. The phrase is a strong one and suggests that before man's knowledge the universe "is not."[1] This must not be misunderstood. The universe *is,* of course; it exists independently of man's knowledge of it. But as so existing it is imperfect, its meaning is potential only, its message is dumb, unexpressed. Now, it is precisely the privilege and dignity of man's intelligence that while being itself it can also "become" in a way other things.

"Being is twofold: material and immaterial. By material being, which is limited, a thing is merely what it is: this stone is just a stone and nothing more. But by immaterial being, which is vast and, as it were, infinite since it is not limited by matter, a thing is not only what it is but in some fashion other things as well."[2] Man's intellect is immaterial; it can in a sense "become" other things. But the beauty of the Thomistic conception is that by thus "becoming" other things it not only realizes its own advance in perfection, but also imparts perfection to the material world itself. By means of knowledge the human mind plays a providential role, shedding on the darkness of the world its own light, and expressing for creation the secrets that are in its breast. The human mind is mediator between the material universe and God: it is, as Aquinas

---

[1] *Nihil est eorum quae sunt ante intelligere.* In 1 Met., e. 1 and 2.
[2] In 2 *De An.*, C. 5.

forcibly puts it, the divinely appointed "remedy" for the imperfection of an order of things that permeates the human organism.

The various sciences are perhaps the first to strike us as an effort on the part of man to redeem the world from apparent chaos. In reality, men were poets and philosophers before they were scientists. But in the modern man's approach to the world, the sciences, which have made such progress since the sixteenth century, bulk very large. At one time it was thought, indeed, that these various sciences, ultimately reducible to physical science, would unaided conquer the universe for mind. Today that vain hope has been interred forever. All that can be said of the particular sciences, ranging from Physics to Psychology, is that they represent merely partial conquests. But no matter how successful or enticing the sciences may appear, the human mind will not easily surrender its birthright to explore not only the various approaches of the particular sciences, but will take all reality for its province. Sooner or later the student of science must feel cramped and fettered if his mind is not allowed to ask all the questions that the universe suggests. "The farther science has pushed back the limits of the discernible universe," writes the German philosopher, Eucken, "the more insistent do we feel the demand within us for a satisfactory explanation of the whole."

Philosophy is nothing more or less than the ultimate form which the desire to know, partially satisfied by science, inevitably assumes. It is the more embracive form of science whose function it is, as the psychologist, Wundt, expresses it, "to unify in one consistent system all the knowledge brought to light by means of the several special sciences and to trace back to their first principles the methods in common use in those sciences and the conditions which they in common assume as prerequisites to all knowledge." At the heart of this expansive and ever-widening desire of knowledge there is the instinct that reality is ultimately some kind of unity in harmony. The world presents itself to all of us as made up of many diverse elements, yet it seems a universe, a one-in-many. Philosophy is simply that ultimate form which science assumes in its effort to seize this unity, to focus all the scattered rays of knowledge on the whole, and to think the universe in an all-embracing synthesis. "All that exists, as contemplated by the human mind," wrote Newman, "forms one large system or complex fact. . . . Now it is not wonderful that, with all its capabilities the human mind cannot take in this whole vast fact at a single glance, or gain possession of it all at once. . . . Or again as we deal with some huge structure of many parts and sides, the mind goes round about it, noting down, first one thing, then another, as best it may, and receiving it under different aspects, by way of making progress towards mastering the whole. . . . These partial views are called sciences . . . they proceed on a principle of division of labour. . . . As they all belong to one and the same circle of objects they are one and all connected together; as they are but aspects of things they are severally incomplete in relation to the things themselves, though complete in their own idea for their own respective purposes; on both accounts they at once need and subserve each other. And further, the comprehension of the bearings of one on another and the use of each to each, and the location and limitation and adjustment and due appreciation of them all, with one another, this belongs, I conceive, to a sort of science distinct from all of them and in some sense a science of sciences, which is my own conception of what is meant by philosophy."

This outlook on the world which sees it as one great system, as a unity, is the unconscious possession of plain man and scientist alike. It is the demand that every thinking being makes upon the universe in which he lives. No matter how dwarfed he may feel before the massed forces of his world, no matter how abashed he is in presence of all its cosmic greatness, a man is greater than the world by the majesty of his thought. He can "think" the universe, contain it in his thought, and if his power of foresight and his capacity to utilize its forces for his own benefit is more immediately a guarantee of his greatness, the ultimate source of all his prerogatives is that by thought he possesses a secret unpossessed by the material world which makes of him, after a fashion, the controller of the world's inherent laws.

Philosophy alone can supply the true credentials for this authority of man. Side by side with the varied and analytic studies of the sciences, philosophy must stand to examine the very conditions of the meaning and intelligibility which the sciences presuppose to be present in the world and which no scientist has the time to examine. All knowledge, every knowing effort, whether of the plain man or of the scientist, postulates something about the world of which the plain man is sublimely unconscious and which scarcely interests the scientist at all. This something about the universe, without which there could be neither the humble knowledge of the man in the street nor the more pretentious science of the scientist, constantly occupies the thought of the philosopher. "Why there is order at all in the universe," says M. Bergson, "and not chaos, is the main problem for a thinking mind."

"There is a deep-seated need in the human mind," very aptly writes another modern thinker, "the roots of which strike far beneath all other needs and interests. This is the need to feel at home in the universe. From this source spring all philosophies." In a world that is thought of as radically chaotic, a plaything of gods with human passions, the result of blind capricious chance, disjointed and disordered, there is absolutely no question of feeling at home. The average man unconsciously makes himself at home, the scientist treats his world with a familiarity the offshoot of which is his power of foresight, and when both awaken to ultimates they must become philosophers or be satisfied to sleep in their unconscious, though very comfortable, positions. Philosophy is simply an effort to awaken fully, a courageous attempt to face *all* the problems, to think them out to the end, even with the knowledge that there will be no end so far as full and final comprehension is concerned.

It is not the way of knowledge to build itself up piece by piece. Psychologists are becoming more conscious day by day that knowledge is an affair of first impressions that are global or structural in character. The child has a terrifying impression of an ugly face before it grasps the details that go to make or mar such a countenance. Knowledge, in fact, progresses from the abstract to the concrete instead of going from the concrete to the abstract: it takes all in at once, the details come later like stars that emerge from the background of the firmament at night. At the back of all man's efforts to know there is the like-impression of the wholeness of the universe. It is this impression, this feeling of being at home in the world, which ultimately is the source of all human knowledge. But as this elementary feeling is already an instinctive philosophy, the source, as that modern writer put it, of all philosophies, it is abundantly evident that instinctively the plain man and the scientist are philosophers.

Every attempt to know, in fact, no matter how humble or limited it may appear, is inspired by this instinctive faith in the ultimate ordering and harmony of reality. The scientist simply cannot abide by isolated facts, no more than Newton could when he thought of gravitation, and he is ever anxious to reduce experience to certain periodicities, recurrences, or laws. Taken all together the sciences are a concentrated attack on isolated facts in an effort to conquer the realm of apparent chaos, an attack inspired by instinctive faith. But the plain man in his simplest judgment employs the selfsame instinctive faith. His humblest affirmations have reverberations throughout the universe at large. There is a whole philosophy, in fact, in every single human judgment.

For fear of making this abstruse, let me remind the plain man that in every effort to know, an attitude to the universe is implied. That attitude is one which demands that there is order and meaning in it. For if reality as a whole had no meaning, then no particular aspect of it could enlighten. Every effort to know is inspired then by an attitude to the whole, which is simply what is meant by philosophy. Every act of knowledge is an instinctive philosophy in action. What that philosophy will be is another question, but for the moment it is clear that *a* philosophy is in question.

If we take a single judgment, such as "chalk is white," we are affirming something (whiteness) of something (chalk). To put it bluntly, we are affirming being, or something that appears real of something real. From first to last the plain man's thinking is about being of some kind. Even when he thinks of "nothing" he has affirmed being twice over, first, that it is, and then, that it is not. But to affirm being is to take up a position in regard to all reality, for beyond being evidently there is nothing. In every act of thought, of knowledge, then, the plain man must plead guilty to a philosophy, to an instinctive philosophy.

That this instinctive philosophy may be justified is not difficult to see. But in that justification a man must pass from unconscious to conscious philosophy. For this "being" which is in question must be intelligible and have meaning. For if being is meaningless, then all things necessarily are devoid of meaning since they belong to being. Either being is knowable, therefore, or nothing can be known, for everything that is known must be grasped as articulated being or some form of being. It is one thing, of course, to say that reality is knowable and must have meaning, and another to hold that the human mind is just the one intelligence destined to exhaust that intelligibility and meaning. To put it another way, it is one thing to know that reality can be known, and another to claim to know the whole of it.

Some years ago it was fashionable to take refuge in Agnosticism. The agnostic usually was not one who confessed he did not know, but who went much further and said that reality could not be known. The chief realities excluded were the real nature of things themselves, the immortality of the soul, and God. Kant was a philosopher of the Unknowable, as was also Spencer. The modesty of Agnosticism was false and ultimately suicidal. For if the real is naturally unknowable, then nothing could be known. And if a limited intelligence did not know the real, especially that form of it associated with physical science, this was no ground for saying that the real was in itself unknowable. If reality is unknowable, then nothing can be known at all. Is reality so unlike itself as to resemble itself in absolutely nothing? For that is the pretension of the agnostic. To say that there are regions of reality beyond human experience which are utterly unknowable is to say that being is so unlike itself as to be not itself, entirely equivocal in meaning. But being must be itself, no matter what demands that theory will make upon the human intellect so prone to deal with the monotony of univocal concepts. I am not now going to open up the difficult question of the analogical significance of being, except to reiterate that every step in the conquest of the universe by knowledge involves an implicit faith that the universe can be known. Plain man and scientist will, and must, grant that.

The conclusion, then, seems warranted that the only alternative lies between a philosophy that is instinctive or unconscious and a philosophy that is conscious. If a man wants to be fully human, if he thinks at all, then he must choose the latter alternative; he must let his thinking light up, as far as possible, his fundamental attitudes. Whatever about the poet, the philosopher is not born, he is man in the making. If there are not more philosophers among the plain men, the reason is that the race of real men, under the pressure of economic needs and other obstacles, is disappearing from our midst. Towns and cities are crowded with individuals who prefer to be gabardined in patches picked up at random from the press, the radio, the public orator, than clad in the rough homespun of their own thinking.

It is related of the old Greek philosopher, Diogenes, that he was once observed traversing the streets of Athens, armed with a lantern as he searched the market-place for something. As he raised his lantern to the faces of the passers-by, one curious person asked him what he sought. "I seek a man," replied Diogenes. But was he not surrounded in that market-place by men of every type and condition: purple-clad nobles and humble artisans passed beneath his lantern? The story is pathetically human for, whatever the intentions of Diogenes may have been, there is a point in it. If it is just his capacity for thinking that marks off man from the rest of creation, just as it is the necessity under which he labors to multiply his thoughts and reasonings that differentiates him from God and angel, then man can be fully human only when he has begun to think for himself and allows the sleeping philosopher in him to come to life.

Philosophy is a human thing: it is a necessity for the human spirit. As Aristotle argued, either a man wishes to philosophize or he does not. If he wants to, then do not stop him. But if he does not wish it, he will have to all the same, if for no other reason than to show he need not. Whether he will it or not then, a man is forced toward some form of philosophy, and without knowing it, like the character who spoke prose unwittingly, every man is a philosopher. But it is a sorry compliment to any man to tell him he is what he knows not himself to be: the unconscious in man's attitudes has always brought upon it the satire of society.

As first employed, the philosopher was looked upon as a friend or follower of wisdom which the Greek word for philosophy evidently conveys. Subsequently, philosophy came to stand for wisdom alone. Now wisdom has never narrowed down its connotation to science or knowledge only, it has always embraced an attitude toward life and conduct. In so far as this is so, the concept of wisdom brings philosophy nearer to the plain man. There may be some excuse for his failing to grasp the philosophic import of his efforts to know, but there is no escape from the philosophy implied in his efforts to live. The task of life is not the monopoly of philosophers: it is for all. Every man is involved by it and every man must have sufficient light to guide his steps. If he take a step at all he must move in some direction, and since every man is moving, the direction of his goal is implied in every step. Man's every action, in a word, is inspired by a philosophy of life and by a faith in the meaning of his life.

## 2

# Philosophy and Life

The attempt of science to solve all problems by scientific concepts constitutes an epoch in the history of human thought. Prior to 1870, scientists hoped to explore the universe, to light it up, and to hold in their hands the formula of its constitution. Physical science stood for absolute knowledge; its concepts were stretched so as to include all domains of reality. As Emile Boutroux phrased it, science had become the old-time metaphysic. But if science had become philosophy, then philosophy was swallowed up by science.

Since then the course of science has changed. It has abandoned the colossal hope to be exhaustive. It no longer takes the nature, origin, or ultimate destiny of the universe for its province: its aims are much more restrained. Sir James Jeans concludes a best-seller on the modest note: "So that our main contention can hardly be that the science of to-day has a pronouncement to make, perhaps it ought rather be that science should leave off making pronouncements; the river of knowledge has too often turned back upon itself."[1]

It is not easy, however, for scientists to "leave off making pronouncements." While science has abandoned its erstwhile ambitions, particular scientists forget the fact, and it is rather typical of every new scientific discovery or interest that it wants to enlarge itself and extend its newly found concepts so as to embrace the facts of existence and of human life. "Only a science which is directly related to life," said William James, "is really a science at all." But what is liable to be forgotten is that no *particular* science can of its very nature hope to embrace all the facts of human life. The problem of life cuts right across the scientific attitude. It is a problem of every man and must be met, as it were, from the outset by scientist and non-scientist alike. But it is the universal science, philosophy, which alone can satisfactorily hope to solve it.

In mid-nineteenth century the German thinker, Eucken, was calling attention to this. When he said that the farther back science has pushed the limits of the discernible universe, the more insistent do we feel the demand within us for a satisfying explanation of the whole, he was really thinking of the oldest and newest problem of all, the problem of life. "The old eternal problems," he says, "rise up before us and clamour loudly and ever more loudly for some newer and better solution. The solution offered by a bygone age was soothing at least, if it was not final. In the present age, however, the problems reappear with an acuteness that is almost painful: the deep secret of our own human nature, the question of our origin and destiny, the intermeddling of blind necessity and chance

---

[1] *The Mysterious Universe*, p. 150.

and pain in the strange, tangled drama of our existence: are not these all so many enigmas which torment and trouble us whithersoever we turn? And all seem to circle around the one essential question: Has human nature a real meaning and value, or is it so utterly amiss that truth and peace will never be its portion?"

Who, by thinking, can hope to create sufficient light to know the self that throbs in human life and makes of it so inalienably a man's own torment or delight? Thinking does but add to the misery of life and serves but to produce a brow "sicklied over with the pale cast of thought." For life is a large thing, an experience so full that thought cannot hope to imprison life's fullness in its bosom: life is larger than thought. It is the story of deep desires, of human endeavors, of a heart throbbing in hate and love, of a spirit rich with feeling and expansive with emotion. The universe around it now thrills, now breaks upon its song, offers itself rough-hewn to be broken and remade, and affords a refuge from the torment of its thought: a man can work at least and cease to think. For if thinking does but intensify life's anguish, then why not live and think not?

With a certain semblance of righteous indignation Carlyle is said to have reversed the motto of the ages: *Know thy work* is his substitution for *know thyself*. In justice to Carlyle it must be said that his motto has been wrenched by many from a wider context. "A certain inarticulate self-consciousness," he writes, "dwells dimly in us; which only our works can render articulate and decisively discernible. Our works are the mirror wherein the spirit first sees its natural lineaments. Hence too the folly of that impossible precept, know thyself; till it be translated into this partially possible one, know what thou canst work at. . . ."[2]

True enough. The inarticulate consciousness that is in the mind of every man shows itself in life. If the ideal is to know what one can work at, then why not get about knowing our life itself? Life is not exhausted by work as commonly understood, and men have leisure for life itself, if they choose to use it. But leisure normally is looked upon as another kind of work which consists in getting as far away as possible from the human self. Men divide their lives between work and play, and leave no margin for self-thought. Hamlet decidedly is out of fashion, but the thought expressed by Hamlet can never lose its force. For

> What is a man
> If his chief good and market of his time
> Be but to sleep and feed? a beast, no more.
> Sure, He that made us with such large discourse,
> Looking before and after, gave us not
> That capability and godlike reason
> To rust in us unused.

The fact of the matter is that every man has a certain number of notions and ideas, a system which determines his outlook, and these ideas go to form what may be called his philosophy of life. Every man has a philosophy in some shape or form, he has a more or less dumb sense of life's meaning, and his general attitude to life betrays his instinctive philosophy. Were Diogenes to come again among us, to renew his quest, it is certain that he would discern in every man a philosopher of kinds. It may be

---

[2] *Sartor Resartus*, p. 112.

granted that this ubiquitous philosopher may be found only half-awake, blear-eyed and semi-conscious, but his presence could not be denied. If the impulse to know, as has been shown, is itself inspired by an instinctive philosophy of the universe, it is much more evident that the effort to live is inspired by some secret philosophy. There is not a single man in any city who does not adopt some attitude to life. That attitude may be inconsequent and inconsistent; it may be such as to cause distress to the logical philosopher in him. It may be elastic enough to stretch from hard work in the noonday to rather plenteous libations in the evening; it may hold within its bosom moods contradictory and warring with one another. But in the dim twilight of the subconscious vision of the most inconsequent individual, there is an attitude to life.

There is not, in fact, a single human being under any sky who does not take up some posture in regard to life. He may stand up to life, or he may take it lying down; he may play and frolic with it, or he may while it away to the tune of *Lazybones*. But escape an attitude to life a man may not. If one in a thousand is subtle or clever enough to suggest that he is committed to no particular attitude, then out of his own mouth he may be condemned: the policy of no attitude is itself an attitude.

"I know," wrote that shrewd psychologist, William James, "that you, ladies and gentlemen, have a philosophy, each and all of you, and that the most interesting thing about you is the way in which it determines the perspective in your several worlds. You know the same of me. . . . The philosophy which is so important to each of us is not a technical matter: it is our more or less dumb sense of what life honestly and deeply means."[3] It is from this instinctive attitude, when unchecked, that springs the whole range of a man's activities. For as a man's humblest efforts to know arise from implicit trust in the order of the universe, so his actions are always somehow an appeal to the inner essence of his universe. The man who consistently cheats his neighbor, by a kind of second nature, believes that life's inner essence is tortuous and twisted; his God, as can be understood, is the supreme Quack.

A man's instinctive philosophy runs in his veins, it pulsates through his every action, it ends by outlining his life as a whole. "There are some people — and I am one of them," writes G. K. Chesterton, "who think that the most important thing about a man is still his view of the universe. We think that for a landlady considering a lodger it is important to know his income, but still more to know his philosophy. We think that for a general about to fight an enemy, it is important to know the enemy's number, but still more imperative to know the enemy's philosophy."[4] A man's life is the testament of his philosophy.

To realize the truth of this, one has only to advert to the elementary distinction between right and wrong which is the possession of the most primitive minds: the unethical man in this respect has yet to be discovered. What in the concrete may be considered right and wrong may vary from individual to individual within certain broad limits. But that there is a right way of living, and a wrong way, is so instinctive that men never question the fact. In that distinction, once the light that it throws on

---

[3]*Pragmatism*, p. 3.
[4]*Heretics*, Preface.

life is followed faithfully, lies a whole philosophy of conduct. Further, why right must be done at all, and wrong avoided, may carry one very far toward framing a system of philosophy. Just as in the humblest efforts of knowledge there was a far-reaching reference to the ultimate constitution of the universe and an implicit faith in it as a whole, so in every trivial action that is properly human is there a philosophy of life which cannot be radically dissociated from the actions that it inspires.

Life, it is said popularly, is action. If we take action in the minimal form which it must assume, not to take too much for granted, it is clear that behind all human activity we can discern a will-action of some kind. In the early stages of the child's life human action is not as yet properly human: it is simply a question of inter-action between the child and its environment. But when the child reaches the point in his life when he may be said to be master of his fate, then decisions of his will may be said to pulsate through his life. Action then becomes so vital a thing that it becomes entirely unavoidable. Even when he wills not to act, or to shirk the duties that life places upon him, he is acting all the same: the will not to act is as obviously a form of action as the will to act.

The moment this is clearly seen, and is admitted, a philosophy of life is already implied. It ought not be difficult to prove this. Human action implies an end to be obtained or a purpose which inspires it. Even when a man apparently acts to no particular purpose, when he enjoys himself at play or recreation, yet even here he has not emancipated himself from the necessity of end or purpose. A man may just perform certain actions for the sake of action, or as an escape from serious occupations, he may play for the sake of play, or with a view to recreating himself. But he cannot empty an action, which is action, of what all action as a form of movement necessarily implies. Philosophically, movement, of course, is a broader notion than merely local movement through space: it is a qualitative change from a potential state of being to its corresponding act and perfection. But all potentialities are faced toward definite actualities: one does not pluck figs from thorn bushes, or gather grapes from cabbage stalks. The end, or perfection, is already indicated by the nature of the potentiality in question. But even local movement is not entirely aimless: if one moves at all, one must go in some direction.

All human action, then, may be said to imply end, or purpose, whether such ends are consciously in mind or not. Admit that, and one is forced to grant that a man's most trivial action will take him a long way: the slightest human action has necessarily a reference to an end that is ultimate and final. What that end must be is not now in question, but that human action abuts on an end that is final is as certain as that there is human action at all. It is this ultimate end, in fact, that makes action possible. If a man sits down quietly and tries to seek his way through the maze of psychological motives for his life and action, he must hit the streak of light that will lead him to a supreme Object of his life.

What is the reason for this assertion? It is simply this, that once a man starts going in this direction he cannot stop until he finds a final and sufficient reason why he acts at all. To start out on a series of ends and purposes, where one thing leads to another and that other leads on to something else and something else to a further something else and so on *ad infinitum,* means that one will never act at all. An illustration of the difficulty, in a small way, is supplied by the very intelligent man who sees so many reasons for and against a course of action that he does not act at all: he is undecided. But that is only an illustration, because fundamentally there is one form of indecision which belongs to no man at all: even indecision covers a decision not to act. Natively we are actually involved in the series of ends and purposes, and that is so because our series of ends is not without its fulcrum and its fixed point from which the series is suspended. Every action, then, bears within it reference to a supreme object in life, and whether we are conscious or not of that hidden relation, the philosophy which it implies is already working at the heart of our lives.

In every man there is the impulse to do and be, to develop and grow, to perfect and realize himself in some way. All his activities, of no matter what color or order, are aspects of this generic impulse that rules his life as a whole. How best to realize his end in life is always dimly present in a man's deep consciousness, for it is already imbedded in his every action. That is implied in a man's moral attitude, no matter how loose or unsatisfactory that attitude may actually be. Little as a man may be aware of it, his instinctive attitude to what for him constitutes the supreme good in life is already operative. That supreme good may be not as yet in full light, no more than the consciousness of ultimate harmony may be in his efforts at knowledge, but even in the shadows it is the supreme good which, like a magnet, is drawing him through the zigzag course of life.

A man's philosophy of life is nothing more or less than this deep attitude of his to what for him constitutes the supreme object in his life. It goes with him all through life, it is the secret source of all his attitudes and activities, and on last analysis the only alternative for him is consciously to be a philosopher, with a theory of life, or unconsciously to be a philosopher and go through life without being aware of the fact. The only alternative, then, in regard to life, as in regard to knowledge, is between a conscious or an unconscious philosophy.

As man's special prerogative is thought, however, it does seem certain that a philosophy which is merely unconscious is not worthy of him. Blind, instinctive action ought not to be man's reaction to life, seeing that he is endowed by thought to guide him. The transition from one's instinctive philosophy is here even more imperatively demanded than in man's attitude to knowledge. Man's moral character is at stake, for whereas animals are led by instinct to act for ends they know not in their character of ends, man is endowed by reason freely to elect for certain courses of action. Properly to select such lines of action, however, a man must light up his life and see the goal he wishes to attain: his more or less instinctive attitude must be replaced by a conscious philosophy which will preside over his endeavors. This is all the more convincing that for moral conduct proper one needs knowledge. Virtue and knowledge are not, as Socrates is supposed to have held, identical. But no man can be really moral by chance. Ignorance and innocence are not one and the same thing from the moral viewpoint, and one whose conduct is morally good, without knowing it, is only accidentally so, as it were. A man usually acts his creed in any case, but if his life is to be really human, his creed must be codified and reflexly known. This really cuts across the psychological difficulty of extricating one's motives from the complexity of one's life: it legislates simply for a view of life that will rescue action from instinctive levels and make it intelligent and human.

Philosophy is an effort to take up this fundamental attitude that is instinctive and render it lightsome and conscious. That can be done in no other way than by thought and reflection. If it is objected that thinking only renders life more difficult, then the solution is not to be found in running away from thought into some subhuman, instinctive escape. If thought does not work, that is not the fault of thought, but of men's thinking, and the only solution is deeper, more prolonged, and clearer thinking. Men cannot shirk the duty of thinking. The alternative never is between thinking or not thinking, but between different ways of thinking, some of which are superficial and therefore bad, and others which are deep and obstinate enough to overcome the inertia of laziness that is in every one of us. We are all as lazy as we can be, somebody has said. But nobody has ever said that laziness can absolve us from the duty of thinking.

The place of intelligence in life is unfortunately somewhat obscured at the present day. Intelligence has come to be identified with the reason of certain scientists in the nineteenth century, and as a result it is far from popular. It may indeed be, as Arnold suggests, that it is not Linnaeus or Cavendish or Cuvier who can give us the secret of life, but Shakespeare with his

> . . . daffodils
> That come before the swallow dares, and take
> The winds of March with beauty

or Wordsworth with his

> . . . voice . . . heard
> In springtime from the cuckoo bird
> Breaking the silence of the seas
> Amongst the farthest Hebrides.

Such poetry surely can send us back with strange exaltation to the life that begets it or enjoys it. But even poetry cannot absolve us from seeking light. Philosophers are not always poets, but never was there a poet who was not a philosopher, and even in the poet the creative part of him is intelligence under the sway of feeling. Intelligence is simply the light of life, it is life, a form of life, life as it grows conscious and limpid to its own eyes. Intelligence, and particularly reason, that is, as a "logical and mensurative faculty," is not the only thing in life; there is volition, feeling, and the many other things that go to make the life of man. But intelligence is privileged just because it is the light of life, a light shared by every man, and without which life is dark and meaningless. It is not every man who can command poetic exaltation, or satisfy himself with its intuition of life. Nor can the other elements of life dictate to thought on the plea that they alone constitute life. Devoid of reason and intelligence, the life of man would shrink in poetic exaltation and in feeling to mere biological vitality. Neither need we suppose man's thinking to be angelic or purely spiritual. He thinks with his whole being; and his feeling, too, when it is not isolated and divorced from thought, will make its contribution. Philosophy as a sense of the whole of life takes into account the full context of the human mind, with its many aspects, in its effort to read life's secret. Unless we are to rest satisfied with instinctive action, or seek refuge in an incommunicable intuition, we must relate life to a conscious philosophy which will seek to indicate life's ideal. "An ideal," as W. James points out, "must be something intellectually conceived, something of which we are not unconscious, and it must carry with it that sort of outlook, uplift, and brightness that go with all intellectual facts. Ideals are relative to the lives that entertain them. To keep out of the gutter is here no part of consciousness at all, yet for many of our brethren it is the most legitimately engrossing of ideals."[5] But even "keeping out of the gutter" is itself inspired by some ideal, and until philosophy throws light on the goal of life, there is little incentive for the upward ascent from gutter to real heights. When philosophy has done this service, it will have removed much of the smug complacency that can go with low ideals. The man who thinks he is all that he ought to be is obviously not all that he should be. He may have reached a little hillock, but if he opens his eyes he will see Alps on Alps arise. The world of moral action is as inexhaustible as the universe of knowledge. How infinitely inexhaustible philosophy alone can tell.

---

[5] *Talks to Teachers* (1919), p. 297.

3

# The God of Philosophy

Philosophy is a determined effort to grasp the unity and wholeness of things. It bids a man look beyond the material world for an integral order which embraces all reality, matter itself included; it integrates life's endeavors in a span that stretches out from every passing moment to an end that is supreme and final. Already in the effort to know, this integral order of reality is postulated, and every moment of human life is charged with an interest that is not of time only, but of eternity. These two fundamental things in human experience, knowledge and moral endeavor, involve a philosophic outlook that is frequently hidden beneath the name of common sense. The only difference between common sense and philosophy is that philosophy is common sense become self-conscious: it is one thing to know and another reflexly to know that one knows and why.

Philosophy attempts to focus attention upon the far-reaching implications of the plain man's outlook, it seeks ultimates for all human endeavors, and in doing this it must light up a sphere that extends beyond the margin of the plain man's actual world and beyond the frontiers of time: it introduces him to the region of invisible reality. By so tracing the active efforts of intelligence and will beyond the realm of space and time, philosophy helps men to see that the world of reality, the real, is of unsuspectedly large dimensions and that, while it includes the actual universe of which every man is so vividly aware, its circumference is by no means coincident with the material world. The material universe, in fact, is seen to be only a fringe of the vast world of reality.

Philosophy leads us beyond the material universe for the reason of man's existence. Man, said Aristotle, is essentially a contemplative animal. He is part of a natural order of things, taking his place with other beings that are organic and corporeal, but he is not entirely of that order. There is in him a strange, passionate desire to look beyond the confines of the world in which he lives. "That a scrap of transient life, pinned to this tiny planet and limited by the apprehensions of its imperfect senses and the interpretations of its yet more imperfect mind," it has been said, "should be filled to the brim with a passion for that which lies beyond life — this, even if it only happened once, would present a difficult problem to the determinist. But it happens frequently. . . . Although it is not a truth which we are fond of, something deep within us insists that Mary has chosen the good, the real, the noble part; and that without her steadfast witness to the Perfection she adores, our busy life of becoming would lose all significance."

In this progress of reflection it must dawn upon the plain man that he is a citizen of two worlds. He lives in a world of matter, with which in his body he seems continuous, but his mind opens on a universe of invisible reality. His senses put him in touch with things that can be seen, felt, and heard. But his mind puts him in contact with a reality that has none of these characters, but which is real, though formless, and spiritual. He finds that he is at home in both worlds, for by his intelligence he is able to read off the meanings of things physical and material, but he finds himself persistently drawn to an environment that reaches out beyond the world of matter. For if all his efforts to know even the physical universe imply the larger order of reality for fullest meaning and intelligibility, and if his every moral effort takes him beyond the realm of space and time, he is forced to think of an ultimate environment for the life of intelligence and will which supplies vitality for the conquest of the very limited portion of reality at his disposal. This ultimate environment must have ultimate truth for intellect and the supreme good for will. But this environment is only another name for God, who is Truth and Life. Nothing has final consistency, then, for the human effort to know or to do until God is reached. But that is only one aspect of the philosophic quest: it is a stage on the way to seeing that nothing at all is fully or finally intelligible until God has been reached. The philosopher is one who in all his reasonings finds the ultimates in God: he explains nothing without reference to Him.

In this, of course, I have in mind the ultimate form of philosophy which is called a metaphysic, but philosophy is best illustrated in its most radical form, and until a man has sensed something of metaphysics he cannot boast the title of philosopher. But if philosophy is liable to deter people the word *metaphysics* has even more harrowing associations, so we had better make as little use of the word as possible. In this matter it is not words that count, nor associations that seem aristocratic. The birth of metaphysics, like that of all true philosophy is humble; it does not wait upon the scientist nor upon his vast, intricate discoveries; it takes its rise in the plain man's most modest statement. For every statement has to do with that common notion of *being* to which the metaphysician must always return as to an inexhaustible source. It is the impact of being that awakens intelligence in its desire to enrich itself with reality and that stirs will into action. It is in contact with being that the human mind becomes aware of itself, of its exigencies and its far-flung horizons. That in all its judgments the human mind must affirm being, is already a revelation of itself to itself. The object, being, is without limit, and the mind that thinks being is one with large capacities, made to reach all reality; it is unsatisfied until it comes in sight of God, without whom the world of reality has no roots or meaning. But the infinitude of intelligence's capacities are communicated by it to man's desires. It would be foolish to think of man as a pure spirit, consisting solely of intelligence and will, but we cannot get away from the fact that in all man's active reactions to life, whether in sin or in sanctity, there is something of infinitude. His aspiration is impetuous and inexhaustible; it can find its peace only in the perspective of the totality of all good in a Good Supreme. Let us retain our conclusion, then, that if a man wants to explain anything fully or finally, from the fall of a leaf to the highest flight of poetic fancy, from the simplest affirmation of the plain man's intelligence to the most subtle form of human desire, he must invoke God. The philosopher is one more conscious of God than any other scientific inquirer; he knows that without Him the universe and all within it are no better than half-truths that do not satisfy; God for him is "the thought that lurks in all delight."

This philosophic conviction of God's ubiquity in the sphere of knowledge does not usually come to a man without a certain sense of collapse on the part of the world around him. This explains why many philosophers have been so God-intoxicated that nothing else seemed real. Who does not recall Plato for whom the ideal was real and for whom the actual world was only a series of pictures, like those on a screen, cast upon the foreground of our lives by the ideas? The philosophy of Plato, of course, is under religious inspiration. For him salvation means deliverance from the bondage of sense and a return of soul to the heavenly home to which she belongs and from which, he believes, she came. We can still visualize Socrates and Phaedrus, as portrayed by Plato, carried on the wings of a discussion of love to a vision of the lower heaven and irresistibly carried forward to the highest heaven. "Of the heaven which is above the heavens," says Socrates, "what earthly poet ever did or ever will sing worthily? It is such as I will describe; for I must dare to speak the truth, when truth is my theme. There abides the very being with which true knowledge is concerned; the colourless, formless, intangible essence visible only to mind, the pilot of the soul. . . . Every soul which is capable of receiving the food proper to it rejoices at beholding reality . . . she beholds justice, and temperance, and knowledge absolute, not in the form of generation or of relation, which men call existence, but knowledge absolute in existence absolute." The philosopher, on Plato's theory, is one who in a previous existence saw "beauty in heaven," and when he comes on earth finds beauty as well. The philosopher, says Plato, is one who "is always, according to the measure of his abilities, clinging to the recollection of those things in which God abides, and in beholding which He is what He is. And he who employs aright these memories is ever being initiated into perfect mysteries and alone becomes truly perfect. . . . He forgets earthly interests and is rapt in the divine . . . and when he sees the beauty of earth, is transported with the recollection of the true beauty."

It is quite certain that to attain to a philosophic vision the universe must perform something very like a somersault before one's eyes. In men's unreflective contact with the world around them it is only too true that for them the really real things are the solid things that they touch and feel and see. The universe given to them by their senses does seem solid and stationary, and by a natural sequence of ideas, this real world becomes the standard of all other things, with detriment to those aspects of experience that cannot be seen or felt or touched. For the average man his mind is much less real than his body, his ideas are only dim reflections of his sensations, the ideal world as a whole is only a wraithlike imitation of the universe of chairs and tables and food and drink. What is the result? The world of reality built up by naïve unreflecting common sense is like a vast pyramid with its broad basis of physical reality and a tapering point which illustrates the diminishing realities of spirit, with God somewhere at the point. For if material things impress men whose life is predominantly one of the senses, then the more things are removed from matter the less real are they, and since God is infinitely removed His Reality has decreased proportionately. Philosophy is the laborious effort entailed in inverting this vast pyramid. When the effort has been successfully accomplished the world of reality is seen to be an inverted pyramid whose base now represents the greater reality of God and whose point symbolizes the diminished reality of material things. The net effect on the philosopher who is conscious of this for the first time is that his world has performed a somersault and that he has begun to see the hierarchy of reality only when he has seen his world upside down.

There is a really rapid way of bringing home this necessary reversal to the plain man. He must admit, despite his conviction of the tremendous reality of material things, that God is the most real Being of all. God, in a sense, is the only really Real, for in Him alone is nature identical with existence: His name is "I am Who am." He is the sufficient reason for His own existence, whereas no other being can lay claim to that. Not only is He the really Real, but everything that has reality owes it to Him. Everything has come from Him and is sustained by Him in existence, since His conservation of reality is His creative act continued and prolonged. Does not that suggest immediately that the hierarchy of reality descends from Him and that according as things approach Him in perfection their reality is enhanced? The measure of God's reality among visible things is greatest in man and it diminishes as it descends through the beings that resemble Him less and less until we dip down to the very lowest beings that are material. God is Thought of Thought, yet most real Real. All things else from Spirit down to man, from man to animal, from animal to matter, are decreasing and diminishing degrees of reality.

It is absolutely essential, then, for the plain man to correct his outlook, and instead of taking reality to be primarily matter and then body and then mind and then spirit and then God, he must reverse the process and go the other way. When he does this he will look out on the world of matter through the eyes of philosophy to see that its apparent reality has shrunk considerably and he is no longer impressed by its solidity and consistency. When he has succeeded in doing this his effort will be rewarded with a new vision of the hierarchy and order of things which is the most vital necessity of our day. "Until this prejudice," writes Mr. Watkin in a most suggestive Essay,[1] "in favour of matter against mind, of the lesser against the greater realities, of the shadow against the substance, has been overcome, Western culture will never regain the intrinsic stability which alone can save it from internal disintegration, nor will modern man find the peace for which he is groping, the peace of order. And it can be overcome only by a thoroughgoing acceptance of the hierarchy involved in all religious faith, indeed, in the very existence of mind; in other words, by that reaffirmation of the metaphysical order of being which is, it cannot be emphasized too strongly, our supreme and most urgent need. For lack of vision the people perish. . . ."

When a man has begun thus to see the world inverted he is rewarded by a vision that is our fundamental need. This vision goes back to Plato who described the real as an "imitation" or participation of the ideal and which for

---

[1]*The Bow in the Clouds,* pp. 160 sq.

religious faith is suggested by the account in Genesis of man's creation in the likeness of God. It is the way of human knowledge to build up the universe of the invisible on the pattern of the visible, to regard things spiritual as images of the visible, to speak of human thought and spiritual emotions in metaphors drawn from the physical world. We speak of spirit as breath, of ideas as illuminations, of their genesis as conception, and of their expression as a "bringing forth." In our unconsciousness of the real order of reality we take it that the term of our reference for the use of spirit is the breathing of the winds, for conception and bringing forth of ideas the biology of conception and birth, and that the spiritual again is only a dim reflection of the greater reality associated with physical happenings or biological experience. A classical example of this unreflecting outlook is to be found in the psychoanalysis of our day which purports to explain the heights of man's aspirations in terms of the depths of his biological life which seem so much more real. But all this is based on the fallacy of the pyramid. The reality is just the reverse. If it is possible to apply the metaphor of breath to spirit and the biological analogy of conception and travail to the life of intelligence, the ultimate reason is that the whole material universe is itself a vast metaphor that has its counterpart in the invisible: the physical world, after the Pauline analogy, is an image of things invisible. That being so, the term of reference must be sought in the greater reality and not in the less, so that if conception has a biological significance, the reason must be that first it has a spiritual counterpart. Now God is the supreme Exemplar and in Him must be found the ultimate reality of which all things else are resemblances. If the terms "breath," "conception," "birth," are applicable to human thought, the reason is that they are on last analysis echoes of God's own thinking. And if psychoanalysis is to be met on philosophic grounds it must be made to see that it is not the depths which explain the heights, but that it is on the heights we must seek the ultimate reason for all begetting, for all desire, for all conception. In man himself the hierarchy of his being demands that spirit informs his energy, and lower desires, instead of explaining his spiritual desires, must be explained by them. But it is in God, in a divine fecundity, that we must find the ultimate explanation of life on all its levels and in all its phases.

No man can advance toward his vision without becoming more and more conscious of the place of God in the universe entire. God becomes the very center of things. No philosopher is worthy of the name who does not see God as the One who makes the many intelligible. That which is one in God, says Aquinas, is multiple outside of Him. For the philosopher, God is the Focus of all light. From Him emanate the rays of truth and goodness and beauty that are scattered throughout reality. Until they are traced to God as Fountain and primal Source the vision of the universe is deficient and entirely lacking. Those who do not feel the need of uniting the many rays that play upon their eyes from the universe all around them have not truly awakened to their human dignity. "There are three kinds of men," wrote the Neo-Platonist, Plotinus, "these first who satisfy themselves with things of sense, for whom the good of sense is the *summum bonum,* who see in suffering an evil, in pleasure happiness, and who employ their wits to secure one and avoid

the other; these are the heavy birds who, for having im-
bibed too much of the earth, are weighed down and cannot fly, though nature gave them wings to fly. There are
others who raise themselves a little in virtue of that attraction which beauty exerts over them but who are in-
capable of looking long on high, descend again to baser
actions that at first they essayed to shun. Finally, there is
a third kind, a race divine, endowed with higher powers
and penetrating glance. Their eyes are filled with the
splendor of the ideal world, they raise themselves above
the clouds and fogs of earth, and poised on high they learn
to despise the things of earth and begin to enjoy this
region where they find themselves at home, like the
wanderer who after a long voyage returns to his native
land."

The spiritualism of Plotinus may be exaggerated, but
it is quite true that until man has raised himself from the
level of the senses to the perspective wherein God is the
center, he cannot enjoy a philosophic vision of the world.
For God is central just because He is the really Real. And
if He is the really Real, He must be the Source of all
reality. It follows that everything that can boast reality is
ultimately of God, that there is more of God in any finite
thing than there is of itself. From that it follows that God
is in every happening and event, no matter how insignificant, and that there is necessarily more of God in every
happening than of finite agents. Every event is a reality,
or it is nothing at all. If it is a reality, there is more of
God in it than of the agent that produces it. Nothing can
happen without Him, without His influence. He is in
everything as the Prime Mover of the universe, just as He
is sought after in every truth and desired in every good.

Granted that the universe apparently is the play of chaotic forces, that human wills malignantly interfere, that even spirits play their role, yet as a happening, whether as a physical or spiritual reality, every event, prescinding from moral character of its agents, is of God on last analysis: there is more of God in it than of the agent who brings it about.

Recall further that the material universe is only a portion of the real order, and that time is only a fragment of eternity, then we are forced to see that the happenings of this world around us can find full and final explanation only in a wider context than the physical universe of time and space. Everything that happens must be placed in an integral order, God's own order, if it is fully to be explained. To take any single happening in the world, say, the instantaneous death of an innocent child beneath the wheels of a passing motor car, without looking for the ultimate context of God's divine order, is like taking a single word out of its context in a paragraph and trying to explain the meaning it bore therein. The ultimate context of every single happening is a whole that includes the invisible and the visible, eternity as well as time.

The world, then, may appear immediately chaotic; chance may seem to rule the destinies of men; the wicked may prosper and the just may suffer. But philosophy reveals an order that takes us beyond the physical world and the uncomforting immediate present, and it tells us that only in this integral order may we seek full and final explanations. To us it may not be given to see these final explanations. But we are assured that they exist, and in this assurance lies the basis of our sanity. Pure philosophy needs no revelation to know that God is good and just;

neither does it need to be told of a future life. If cultivated, philosophy can impart a tremendous sense that in God our human values are in safekeeping; with Him they are conserved and ultimately justified. Appearances may be dead against our sense of values, the calamities of life may appear appallingly unjust and cruel, pain and suffering may be quiveringly intense and dazzling to our sanity. The philosopher who has found God, however, is unperturbed upon the heights of his vision, no matter how intense may be the storm that sweeps over the lower levels of his human feeling. He knows that God must triumph, that justice will be upheld, that pain and suffering must fit into an ultimate scheme of things, that even evil must bring forth good. Philosophy lets in the light of meaning upon existence and reveals the scattered events of life as beads upon a thread of purpose. The order that philosophy reveals as implied in man's simple effort to know and do is an order that is backed by God, First Cause and Ultimate Recompense of all moral effort.

# 4

# The Solace of Philosophy

Hitherto we have been considering human life as an active endeavor which reveals itself in man's effort to know and in his desire to shape his conduct in conformity with some standard of human goodness. A new idea makes its appearance in the immediately preceding pages which suggests that in so far as human life presents a passive aspect the only basis of human sanity is to be found in awakening to the full and integral order of reality which is more extensive than the purely physical order of time-sequence in which mortal lives are involved. A real insight into the practical utility of the philosophic outlook, as a solace for human life, is to be sought in the development of this new idea.

It may at first sight seem strange to seek solace from philosophy. To philosophize is to think, and thinking in the eyes of many is the root of all their miseries. It is only when men think that they begin to be troubled by the problems of life and feel

> The heavy and weary weight
> Of all this unintelligible world

upon their brows. To think, it has been said, is to be filled with many miseries, and philosophy and quiet desperation are synonymous for many. "You are a philosopher, Dr. Johnson," remarked a fatuous optimist one day, and he went on to add, "I, too, have tried to be a philosopher, but I couldn't; cheerfulness was always breaking in." But as there is no escape from thinking, the only remedy lies in thinking well and deeply, and if a little thinking leads to desperation, much thinking and well may at last be rewarded. The philosopher in common parlance is one who has acquired the constant mood of equanimity and of comparatively undisturbed acceptance of things as they come.

Life, for a great part, does consist in accepting things. It would be erroneous to look upon life exclusively as a purely active endeavor of knowledge or of moral effort; for life is no such thing. Though action, a will-decision of some kind, we have argued, is the very inner core of life, life is not always the active thing many suppose. Some theorists convey the impression of life as an active endeavor simply, one in which knowledge, love and external action play the fundamental roles:

> All the world's a stage,
> And all the men and women merely players;
> They have their exits and their entrances,
> And one man in his time plays many parts. . . .

Even here we have forgotten that they act who merely sit and wait. For if at the basis of all human life there is a will-decision of some kind, the issue of that decision may be inaction, it may have the force of reducing men to comparative passivity.

Many things simply happen to men and they are necessarily passive before them; they simply register the happenings or experience them. A great portion of human life is taken up with that, with the impact of an external universe, with the intermingling of chance and fatality in their lives, with the influence for good or evil of their fellows upon them. A man's passage through life may not infrequently appear to him as a perilous journey where fortune lies ambushed. It matters apparently little how he carries himself in this passage; the arrows released by fortune are proverbially indifferent in their aim, piercing the good and missing the wicked. But, once pierced by blind fortune, a man is marked for the blows of fellow men; misfortunes never come singly. "Amongst men," said Dryden, "those who are prosperously unjust are entitled to a panegyric, but afflicted virtue is insolently stabbed with all manner of reproaches." It was this conviction which probably inspired him to write the bitter lines that many have felt so true:

> When I consider life, 'tis all a cheat,
> Yet, fool'd with hope, men favour the deceit.
> Trust on, and think to-morrow will repay,
> To-morrow's falser than the former day.
> Lies worse, and, while it says, we shall be blest
> With some new joys, cuts off what we possesst.
> Strange cozenage! None would live past years again,
> Yet all hope pleasure in what remain,
> And, from the days of life, think to receive,
> What the first sprightly running could not give.
> I'm tired of waiting for this
> Which fools us young, and beggars us when old.

Hence, as somebody has said, "all the world is perpetually at work about nothing else, but only that our poor mortal lives should pass the easier and the happier life for that little time we possess them, or else end the better when we lose them."

But are men reduced to waiting simply? It is true that things happen to men, and they must be resigned to have it so, but does not the secret lie in the way in which men take such happenings? Experience is not merely what happens to a man but what he does with what happens to him, and if what he does with them suggests a turning to account of them in the future, the present of their actual happening cannot be overlooked. It is precisely the way in which a man takes the events of his life that counts, and his future will be largely determined by his present version of the things that happen to him.

The conspiracy of chance and fatality in human life, the intermeddling of human agents and natural events, the slings and blows of fortune, are too obvious to be denied. A man of sensitive disposition may be permanently maimed by the shock of such factors; iron enters into the souls of many and makes life bitter. The smart of failure can fester; the frown of fortune may scorch the roots of heroism. One would imagine that on all sides man is exposed to the colossal work of fortune, which can make or mar him. He seems positively to register the impact of a hostile world and to be the plaything of chaotic forces and iniquitous human thwartings. But if man is free, and we believe he is, the plain man accepts the fact unquestioningly, then in his freedom he can turn in their sockets the weapons of fortune or of men, and blunt them. But, before that is possible, he must have the vision of events and happenings that comes from philosophy: in this vision lies the solace of philosophy.

It is not human to be a mere sensitive machine set pas-

sively to register happenings; it is not worthy of man to be hurled from impression to impression or in inactivity to await life's happenings; it is foolish to allow oneself to be jostled and elbowed through life by the force of circumstance or by men in frantic haste. There is a *tide* in the affairs of men, as Shakespeare said, and the happiest warrior has not ceased to be

> . . . the generous Spirit, who, when brought
> Among the tasks of real life, hath wrought
> Upon the plan that pleased his boyish thought:
> Whose high endeavours are an inward light
> That makes the path before him always bright:

Without vision life is a plunge in the dark, the scurrying of wayward cattle, but even high endeavors may have to be bent to the mere acceptance of what cannot be avoided:

> Who, doomed to go in company with Pain,
> And Fear, and Bloodshed, miserable train!
> Turns his necessity to glorious gain;
> In face of these doth exercise a power
> Which is our human nature's highest dower;
> Controls them and subdues, transmutes, bereaves
> Of their bad influence, and thus good receives; . . .

For no man can take refuge in some evil fate that serves no God. That was good enough for the poor, uneducated, superstitious pagan who placed fate above his gods and was happy to scurry through life and escape, if possible, the inscrutable designs of Nemesis.

Is there no outlook that will be broad enough to embrace fate and fortune in one scheme with design and purpose, or make successful wickedness and offended innocence cohabit together, that will preserve men's sanity in a world where chance's ruling is so persistently annoying? It is philosophy's pretension that it can furnish this wide outlook. Should philosophy succeed, then it must be regarded as a man's best friend. For if the surest friend is the one who comes to a man in trial and woe, philosophy is humanity's friend indeed. As long as life is merry, full of joy and frolic, philosophy stands patiently in the distance. But when a man's house is shattered above his head he will find his friend awaiting him on his doorstep. Either then he will take the hand offered to him by philosophy, or he goes out aimlessly into the darkness of despair.

A typical instance of the consolation afforded by philosophy to a man suddenly overtaken by adversity is afforded by that far-off figure of the fifth century of our era Boethius, whose work, *De Consolatione Philosophiae*,[1] was regarded as an oracle throughout the Roman Empire for two centuries and which today, after such a lapse of time, is rightly regarded as a classic. Born in 487, Boethius, while yet a boy, had consular dignity conferred upon him, the Roman people wishing thereby to honor in the son his father, Aurelius Boethius. By 510, Boethius, the son, had become a consul on his own, without colleague. Within twelve years from that he had climbed to the summit of prestige and honor, and as head of administration was privileged to see history repeat itself when his own two sons were proclaimed consuls as a token of esteem for himself, their father. But Boethius was not long to enjoy his honors. By a turn of fortune, by intrigues that it is not

---

[1] Edited by Fortescue, completed by the Rev. Dr. J. Smith, London, 1925. (This edition is in Latin.)

for us now to understand, Boethius fell from his proud eminence; his universe began to tremble about him. Unheard, he was condemned to exile and death. It was in this plight, imprisoned in some place the details of which are not clear except by contrast with his erstwhile sumptuous dwellings, that Boethius wrote the *De Consolatione Philosophiae,* whereby he lives, as he awaited torture and the end.

The way in which the sorrowing and broken Boethius describes his meeting with philosophy is well worth quoting:

"Whilst in silence I recounted these things, and with my pen did delineate my griefs and complaints, a woman of a most reverend countenance seemed to stand over my head, with sparkling eyes, which were of an extraordinary force and quickness; her colour was lively, and her strength seemed to be unexhausted, although she was so old, that she could by no means be thought one of our time. It was difficult to judge of her stature; for sometimes she appeared to be of the common height of men, then she would seem to touch the clouds with her head; which again, when she raised higher, she pierced the very heavens with it, and was not to be followed by the eyes of those who looked after her. . . . So soon as she saw the patroness of poetry standing by my bed, and dictating to me words, she immediately broke out into these expressions: What unwise person has suffered the *scerique* strumpets to have access to this sick man; who are so far from encountering his distemper with specifique and natural remedies, that they only nourish and increase it by those sweet poisons which they infuse. These are they who, with the fruitless thorns of the passions, choke and destroy the hopeful crops of productive reason, and who only accustom the minds of men to bear and endure a disease, but never free them from it."

These details are precious. One would have thought Boethius knew the romantic malady which has driven so many to the luxury of soft poetry when some sterner medicine was needed to stiffen them for the task of life. The upshot of the matter, as portrayed by Boethius, was that in the farthest depths of philosophy's eyes he descried the real horizons of human life and was able to justify the ways of God. The immediate objects that men so avidly sought from life, he learned, were but insignificant installments of some infinitely greater and more sublime Object, the Supreme Good. The things of creation are like scattered rays that scintillate on the surface, and the tragedy of human life is to fill one's eyes with these beauties of an hour and fail to see beyond them. Scattered as they are over a myriad objects, these rays occupy the divided lives of men in quest of success and power, prestige and wealth, health of body and body's pleasure; they produce a temporary blindness that obscures the Sun which from some high unseen fastness sheds its effulgence on their lives, and when adversity comes they starve and grumble in the darkness of their lives. "Arise then, ye miserable slaves, deceived by earth's false grandeurs, and raise your eyes to the ideal, the only final resting-place, the only secure port of refuge for the shipwrecked. The gold that flows in the Tagus or Hermian waters, the rubies illuminated to living flames by the pure sun's rays, serve but to darken still more the infamous darkness of your hearts and to hide the heavens from your corrupted hearts. Burrowed shamefully in the earth, this is the god, Gold, whom you adore. Mortals, if you wish to contemplate the skies, purify your souls from passion."[2]

There is a peculiarly modern ring in that outburst against the golden god and in his preaching to purify our souls. For we can scarcely call our souls our own. If the essence of life, as Jourbet thought, lies in thinking and being conscious of one's soul, the modern mind can scarcely be said to have made a beginning. For it has lost its soul and is very troubled by

> . . . this strange disease of modern life
> With its sick hurry, its divided aims.

Says Wordsworth:

> The world is too much with us; late and soon,
> Getting and spending, we lay waste our powers.

Arnold takes up the theme:

> For what wears out the life of mortal men?
> 'Tis that from change to change their being rolls:
> 'Tis that repeated shocks, again, again,
> Exhaust the energy of strongest souls
> And numb the elastic powers.
> Till having us'd our nerves with bliss and teen,
> And tir'd upon a thousand schemes our wit,
> To the just-pausing Genius we remit
> Our worn-out life, and are — what we have been.

Many experiencing the fever and fret, a disease contagious, dream with Keats of some dull opiate with which to numb their sense of life, re-echoing his words:

---

[2]*Op. cit.,* Bk. III, x.

> . . . for many a time
> I have been half in love with easeful Death,
> Called him soft names in many a mused rhyme,
> To take into the air my quiet breath . . .

Arnold is right in his diagnosis. Many are only

> Vague half-believers of our casual creeds
> Who never deeply felt, nor clearly will'd,

and lives are chaotic when the immediate present rules the impulse, and when life is not animated by

> . . . *one* aim, *one* business, *one* desire.

Why, then, should men await the collapse of things around them to cultivate philosophy? Is there nothing more in life than the satisfaction of pressing, practical needs, or in the heavens nothing but

> . . . Commerce argosies of magic sails,
> Pilots of the purple twilight, dropping down with costly bales?

The anodyne is not to escape from life and in an excess of romantic melancholy dream, to the tune of nightingales' careless rapture, of ceasing

> . . . upon the midnight with no pain,
> While thou art pouring forth thy soul abroad
> In such an ecstasy!
> Still wouldst thou sing, and I have ears in vain —
> To thy high requiem become a sod.

Human lives with no spiritual ideals are less than human, ships tossed helplessly on their course —

> The magnet of their course is gone, or only points in vain
> The shore to which their shiver'd sail shall never stretch again.

It is philosophy in the first instance that looks into life to see mirrored in its depths the far-off horizons of man's ultimate environment. Why not look in time, escape a moment from the atmosphere of melancholy that poets create around the dull, unintelligible world they declare is ours, and avoid the plight of that unfortunate man who at the approach of death gathered hurriedly together a few books to see if he might not find therein the solace of survival and immortality.

Poetry may suggest a view of things when sorrow and pain are no more, when the present world will be merged in the millennium of the poet's dreams. Shelley in *Prometheus Unbound* sees the whole world breaking into music; matter turns into life, the moon sings its resurrection:

> Music is in the sea and air,
> Winged clouds soar here and there,
> Dark with the rain new buds are dreaming of:
> 'Tis love, all love!

But it is the solace of philosophy that it can turn the universe of the present to love's music by revealing an integral order where Love is creative of the whole, where Love impels all living things and where Love mysteriously rewards. Philosophy insists that nothing in the vast context of reality is isolated or capable of separate and final explanation. The order in which we are at present involved is but a portion of the whole and the events of time take place against the background of eternity.

The revelation made by philosophy to Boethius is centuries old, but it is as actual in the twentieth century as it was in the fifth. Toward the end philosophy says to him: "For in this matter men are wont to make questions of the simple actings of providence, of the order and course of destiny, of sudden chance, of knowledge, of divine pre-destination, and of free-will. . . . The generation of all things and every progression of changeable natures, and all things which are any way moved, receive their causes, order, and forms out of the stability and constancy of the divine Mind. And this being placed in the height of its own purity or simplicity, doth establish a manifold mode or way in doing things; which mode or manner of pro-ceeding, when men behold it in the purity of the divine understanding, is called providence; but being applied and referred to that which it moveth, and of which it dis-poseth, is called fate or destiny . . . and although these things be different, yet one of them depends upon the other; for the order of fate proceeds from the pure sim-plicity of providence. . . . This certainly is manifest, that the immovable and simple way of doing things is provi-dence; and that the movable contexture and temporal order of those things which the divine purity fore-dis-posed and ordered to be done, is fate. Hence it is that all things which are under the dominion of fate are also subject to providence, which commands even fate itself. . . . Hence it is that although things may seem confused and disturbed to men who cannot aright consider this order, nevertheless the proper manner and course of everything directs and disposeth it to the true good: For there is nothing done for the sake of evil, no, not by the most flagitious wretches. . . . But thou mayest say, what greater confusion can there be, that both prosperous and adverse things should by times happen to good men, and that evil men can enjoy what their hearts desire and yet be afflicted too with things which they hate? Do people live nowadays so virtuously, and with so much integrity, that those whom men think good or bad, must necessarily be either? . . . It is only the great power of God which can make evil turn to good. . . . For a certain order embraceth all beings, so that whatsoever doth depart from the reason and laws of that order which is assigned to it, yet it passeth into and under the laws of another order; for nothing is left in the power of chance or uncertainty in the realm of providence."[3]

Philosophy keeps in mind the only order that is final and ultimate, the order of all things under God, where chance and fortune subserve, and must promote, God's ends. Chance and fortune as causes which may produce results unthought of or unintended may play their role within the universe as the plain man knows it, but in the order which the philosopher discovers neither chance nor fortune rule, since it is the order of God. In the discovery of this order and in the contemplation of the ultimate perspective, which is that of God, the philosopher seeks, as far as may be, to see the universe through the eyes of God. In that divine vision where evil worketh to good, where fortune favors design, where chance or chaos are no more, lies the solace of philosophy.

---

[3] *Op. cit.,* Bk. IV, 5.

# 5

# The God of Christianity

The path of inquiry into the problem of the universe and human life, lighted up by the torch of reason alone, leads the philosopher to a point where a dim perspective is obtained from which reality and life, so chaotic in the deep valley in which we live, is seen to be possessed of an inherent order and purpose. That perspective is a divine perspective; the philosopher knows that nothing escapes the empire of God's power. As long as we remain imprisoned within the confines of space and time it is as if we were looking simply at a patchwork which, on the other side of the tapestry, makes unity and design. If the philosophy of Boethius was requisitioned for its potential solace, the reason is not to be sought in the fact that Boethius supposedly was a Christian, but rather because he had a philosophic outlook that took him to the heights from which chance and fatality bathed in the light of an all-pervading providence. So devoid indeed of positive Christianity is this particular work of Boethius that many have inferred he was no Christian at all. A negative argument like that proves nothing, and the Christianity of Boethius is fairly well established from other sources.

No matter how convincing, however, the sanity of philosophic vision may be in itself, it is another matter to decide if it will grip the minds of men and women unaccustomed to prolonged reflection. What St. Augustine says of the God of Plato may be applied to the plain man's view of God. "It is one thing," says Augustine, "to behold from some wooded height the land of peace, and another to march thither along the high road." Platonic philosophy was the "wooded height"; it pointed to God, but was powerless to bring man to God. "Where then is your God?" asks a modern writer, "You say, He is everywhere; then show me *anywhere* that you have met Him. You declare Him everlasting: then tell me any moment that He has been with you. You believe Him ready to succour them that are tempted, and to lift those that are bowed down: then in what passionate hour did you subside in His calm grace? in what sorrow lose yourself in His 'more exceeding' joy? These are the testing questions by which we may learn, whether we too have raised our altar to an 'unknown God' and pay the worship of the blind; or whether we commune with Him 'in Whom we live and move and have our being.' "[1]

There is an appeal in words such as these, and one readily calls to mind the experience of the profound French thinker, Pascal, set forth so vividly in a few broken words. His *Memorial,* as it is called, was a scrap of parchment on which, round a rough drawing of a flaming Cross, he wrote a few abrupt, expressive phrases. This document, which was found on his person, has dis-

---

[1]Martineau, J., *Hours of Thought,* Vol. II, p. 8.

appeared, but it is the classical expression of a man dissatisfied with the God of philosophy. Here are the scraps of gasping words: "From half-past ten until a half-hour after midnight, Fire!" "Fire, Fire, Fire," he repeats and so conveys the vivid emotion that came upon him. But it is the following words that are significant:

> "The God of Abraham, the God of Isaac, the God of Jacob,
> Not the God of philosophers and scholars."

The testimony of Pascal is striking; it may be shared by many. But this subjective reaction does not take from philosophy's contribution: it simply says that the "God of philosophers and scholars" did not make the same appeal to Pascal as did "the God of Abraham," the God of religion.

Without losing anything of the ground gained then by rational inquiry, let us see something of the significance of the God of religion for the universe and life. Admittedly, the greatest Exponent of God to man was Jesus Christ, the Founder of Christianity. He brought to the world a characteristic and original solution for the problem of God, which is the central problem of all philosophy. He revealed a concept of God infinitely richer than philosophy had ever dreamed. But in one particular His revelation intensifies the solace that philosophy strives to impart. The God revealed by Christ is One who has come near to man, so near in fact that in Christ He appears a Man among men. But by so entering into humanity He has stepped out of eternity into time. The life lived by Him who was God and Man is a parable for those who philosophize on providence. Many things follow from the

Incarnation, but here we are viewing simply Christ's solution of the problem of all philosophy, the problem of God.

Philosophy without God is in itself the most contradictory of things contradictory; only human blindness could explain a system purporting to be a philosophy without God. So true is this that the existence of a reflecting atheist is in itself a baffling problem. That there are, and have been, men who style themselves atheists is undoubted. But whether the atheism of such men is real, efficacious atheism is more than open to dispute. We have seen that implicitly every man is affirming God in every judgment; the only alternative lies between conscious and explicit affirmation of God and one that is unconscious and implicit. There is no escape from that, and atheism in reality is a testament of unconsciousness on the part of those who embrace it. We are not denying the sincerity or good faith of those who declare that God does not exist; we simply question the degree of consciousness and reflection that accompanies such assertions. It is impossible efficaciously to deny God, and those who do so will be found to worship a god of their own fashioning. God is so vitally necessary to all human thinking that the only way of escape from Him, which is no escape, is to cease thinking altogether. The man who denies God is in no better a position than he who, with truth as he thinks, denies the existence of truth. Remove God and everything must topple, for the atheist who is logical should cease to live, to make any effort, to entertain any desire. Why should he? The objective foundation of moral effort is God; the guarantee of scientific research is God. The effort to live and to know presupposes God, but in their sheer unconsciousness men may mistake many things for the Deity.

Not only has the idea of a Supreme Being of some kind never radically left the minds of common people,

> . . . in even savage bosoms,
> There are longings, yearnings, strivings,
> For the good they comprehend not,
> That the feeble hands and helpless,
> Groping blindly in the darkness,
> Touch God's right hand in the darkness,
> And are lifted up and strengthened

but there never has been a philosopher of any real dimensions who was not forced to invoke God to explain reality and moral effort. Aristotle and Plato represent Greek philosophy at its peak-point: both believed in God. In modern times Kant and Spinoza view God differently, but they believed in Him. Even the German philosopher, Fichte, who in his lifetime was accused of atheism, and who sailed close to the winds of atheism by saying that God is not but is a process of becoming, was not, strictly speaking, an atheist: his theory regarded chiefly the nature of God's reality. Every philosopher who made any effort worthy of note to harmonize a universe of many objects looked to God.

This practical unanimity of the great philosophic minds of history is significant. But there is another aspect of the God of philosophy no less illuminating. That God should know, in virtue of His perfect self-possession, and that He should affirm Himself in love, in a word, that He should possess what men regard as highest value in this life, personality, is a view that has always suggested itself to philosophic minds. Unanimity here is not quite so much in evidence as in the case of God's existence. Many have been frightened by the bogey of anthropomorphism. Ever since Xenophanes scoffed at the Greek mythological accounts of the gods men have been found to imitate his superficial cleverness. "Everyone," said Xenophanes, "pictures the gods as being like himself: the negro thinks of them as black and flat-nosed, the Thracian as fair and blue-eyed, and, were horses and oxen able to paint, they would undoubtedly depict the gods as horses and oxen." The exaggeration of Xenophanes contains its own summary refutation. To speak of a personal God is not exactly the same as speaking of Him as flat-nosed or blue-eyed, and those who do so speak are not quite so unenlightened as Xenophanes would have us think. In any case, the only way to avoid anthropomorphism is to be conscious of it and to sense the limitations of man's concept of God. But if anthropomorphism means that a man thinks as a man, there is no escape: his intelligence is human. Yet by virtue of intelligence, man has an escape from his human limitations: it puts him in contact with reality. When a man argues that personality, which is a positive perfection, is realized in God, he does not pretend to determine how God is personal; he has sense enough to know that if personality is realized in God it is realized in God's own way and not after a human fashion. Philosophy declares God mysterious, and how Godhead and personality go together no philosopher dare explain. But that there is one God and that this God is a personal God is the conclusion of all sane philosophy. If a philosopher cannot explain the coincidence of these two notions in God, especially when he knows that God is a mystery, then it is a bad policy to let go of one truth to safeguard another truth, or dogmatically to state that because God is one, He is one Person.

In all antiquity there was no nation on the face of the earth that held the unity of God with the same tenacity as did the Jewish people through its checkered history. Yet, when God chose to reveal Himself, Christ was born in the midst of this very people. He was born of a Jewish Virgin, with Jewish ancestry, and in the obscurity of the little town of Bethlehem. His conception by the power of the Most High was miraculous and conceived by Mary according to His human nature, Christ did not cease to be the eternal Word of God. In Christ two natures, divine and human, were united together, but the Subject of this union was the Person of the eternal Son of the Father. "And the Word was made flesh, and dwelt amongst us, and we saw his glory, the glory as it were of the only begotten of the Father, full of grace and truth."[2]

When Jesus Christ emerged out of the obscurity of His early life it was as a Man among men, One who had been brought up in the traditions of His race and who spoke the language of His people. But from the very moment of His appearance there was a something about Him that made His contemporaries admit that no one had ever spoken as He had;[3] the challenge of His sinlessness was unanswerable; He had done things that were impossible if God were not with Him.[4] He taught His doctrines in

[2]John 1:14.
[3]John 7:46.
[4]John 3:2.

images and parables; He summoned a little band to His side to educate them in His outlook. But the process of educating them proved a slow one. Peter had a flash of illumination that made him confess Christ's divinity; not one of them fully grasped His mission; toward the end He avowed that as long as He had been with them they knew Him not.[5] The Spirit that He would send would teach them.

What was the central thing in Christ's solution of the problem of God? Jesus Christ, of course, was not merely a philosopher who elaborates a system and codifies his tenets, though His doctrine does contain an intellectual content. His doctrine in the first instance was Himself: He stood for something that was utterly difficult for the Jews to accept. When He told the disciples that they knew Him not, He put His finger on their difficulty and on His own contribution. "He that seeth Me seeth the Father, for I and the Father are one."[6] He was an Incarnation of God, God's Revelation in time. He was the Bridge between divinity and humanity. In Him divinity had lowered the heavens, and earth had leaped to Godhead. He was therefore the Approach for men to God. But Christ, though identical in nature with the Father, was distinct in Person: He was the Son. The original thing in His account of God, then, is the Fatherhood of God.

In the acceptance of Christ lies the hope of a sonship not unlike His own. He never makes Himself in His lifetime merely one of men. His Sonship is unique, infinitely removed, an eternal begetting by the Father, but in

---

[5]John 14:7.
[6]*Ibid.*

time men will become sons of God by a participated sonship, accepting Christ and opening their souls for the
Life that He will share with them in His death and resurrection. St. John, having witnessed to the Incarnation,
goes on immediately to add: "As many as received Him
He gave them power to be made sons of God, to them that
believe in His name,"[7] and St. Paul puts the matter strikingly when he says: "For whom He foreknew He also
predestinated to be made conformable to the image of His
son; so that He might be the first-born of many brethren."[8]

This Fatherhood of God, therefore, is the original thing
in Christianity. That in the Old Testament there was
some glimpse of it will be clear from Isaiah's prophecy,
some eight centuries before the advent of Christ, when he
speaks of God as Emmanuel, God in the midst of men.
That the Hebrew people, because of God's special predilection, had some idea of it is also clear. But the meta-
phorical way of speaking on the part of this people really
looked forward to the fact which gave it meaning, the
coming of Christ and the sharing of His life with men,
and further, the Fatherhood of God in its real ontological
sense was extended by Christ to *all* men who would accept
Him, and not exclusively to the chosen people.

Hidden in this revelation of God is something astound-
ingly new for all thought outside the revelation made by
God, something that philosophers could scarcely entertain. Aristotle could well see the ascent of all creation, the
striving too of humanity, toward the heights where God
dwells. A modern interpreter puts it well: "Are you
sure," asks Philonous in M. Jacques Maritain's *Theonas,*

[7]John 1:12.
[8]Rom. 8:29.

"that you are right in saying that Aristotle held the life of contemplation to be a superhuman life? Was it not rather for him the life of man most fully human?" Theonas replies: "It would be better to say that for him it was both at once; and it is precisely in this that he seems to me to have seen most deeply into our nature." In man philosophers have recognized a passionate desire to see beyond, to look, to contemplate reality in the light of God. Plato also surmised the aspiration of the human mind to traverse the hierarchy of beauty up to the heights and out beyond to behold the Ocean of uncreated Beauty. For, according to Plato, the soul remembered the glory of its previous existence: "There was a time," said Plato, "when Beauty was clearly manifested to us, when in the train of Zeus or of some other god we saw the glorious vision and were initiated into the most blessed of all mysteries." The sight of beauty then awakens Eros, or love, in man's soul and from beauty to beauty he is impelled toward Plato's highest empyrean. "When anyone," says Plato, "having the right kind of love, mounts up and begins to see the beauty present in the beautiful person, he is not far from the final goal. For the right way of love, whether one goes alone or is led by another, is to begin with the beautiful things that are seen here, and ascend ever upwards aiming at the beauty that is above, climbing, as it were, on a ladder, from one beautiful body to two, and from two to all the others, and from beautiful bodies to beautiful actions, and from beautiful actions to beautiful forms of knowledge, till at length from there one reaches that knowledge which is the knowledge of nothing other than Beauty itself, and so knows at last what Beauty really is. And when one has attained thither,

O Socrates, said my Mantinean friend, there if anywhere is the life that is worth living, in the beholding of Beauty itself." This is subsistent Beauty, the Beauty that really is, "eternal, which neither comes into existence nor passes away, which suffers neither growth nor decay."

Both Plato and Aristotle are vividly conscious of the ascent of man, the stretching out after God of what is noblest in him. But what is lacking is just the thing that is so dominant in Christ's conception. For, as revealed by St. John and as borne out by Christ's own life, the secret of Christianity is the stooping down of God, the descent of God in love, a love on the part of God for man distinct enough from man's love for God to need a new word in Greek to convey its meaning. *Eros* was the word of love employed by Plato and Aristotle; *Agape* is the word employed by St. John. In St. John's Gospel and three Epistles love, or *Agape,* is the constant theme. "For God so loved the world, as to give His only begotten Son; that whosoever believeth in Him may not perish, but may have life everlasting."[9] The love of the Father is brought to earth by Jesus Christ: "But that the world may know, that I love the Father: and as the Father hath given Me commandment, so do I: Arise, let us go hence."[10] When Christ Himself gave proof of love to men, it was in the name of the Father. "Greater love than this no man hath, that a man lay down his life for his friends. . . . But I have called you friends: because all things whatsoever I have heard of My Father, I have made known to you."[11] This downward descent of God into men was the love of God, the Father loving the Son, and the Son loving hu-

[9]John 3:13.
[10]John 14:31.
[11]John 15:13-15.

manity. "As the Father hath loved Me, I also have loved you."[12] Nor must there be any obstacle placed in the way of this outpouring of divine love; it must inundate the whole universe of men. "A new commandment I give unto you, that you love one another, as I have loved you."[13] The love of man for man must resemble the self-less, generous *Agape* of God. "For God is charity: and he that abideth in charity, abideth in God, and God in him."[14]

Had philosophers realized it, they would have seen that the upward ascent, or *Eros,* of the human spirit to God was in itself the reverse side on a lower plane of God's *Agape.* God could not create a being that would not be impelled toward Him, since He is the Goal of all things. But since God was in Himself entirely self-sufficient, He had no need to create at all. All creation is a form of *Agape* or divine love. But philosophers did not see that, because they had no idea of the concept of creation. But the Incarnation, with its revelation of God's Fatherhood, and the taking up of humanity into a participated sonship with Christ, is an infinitely greater form of divine love: the consequences, accordingly, are infinitely more striking.

If the solace of philosophy, then, lies in its revelation of an integral order of things that is backed by God, the revelation of God made by Christ to humanity introduces us to a view of things that sees God's boundless love in all life's happenings. Christ has merely to look at the lilies of the field, more gloriously garmented than even Solomon, to be reminded of His message: the Fatherhood of

---

[12]John 15:9.
[13]John 14.
[14]1 John 4:16.

God. He looks into the air and sees the birds that work not and yet are cared for; even the little sparrow cannot fall from its nest without God. He looks into the heart of man and says that no father will hand his child a scorpion instead of bread; He hears the opening of a door in the night to the impetuous knocking of a visitor and points the lesson; He pictures the father who runs to greet the prodigal. . . . That is the kind of God that Christ revealed. The Christian is one who has faith enough to accept the God of Christ, a God who loves him.

# 6

# Philosophy and the Faith

Whether we view life as a speculative inquiry or as an active endeavor the only alternative seems to lie between a philosophy that is conscious and an outlook that is little more than one of instinct. When that partial passivity which is forced upon us by the universe and by fellow men is taken into account, instinctive reactions will no longer work: we need a conscious vision to ensure our sanity. If this is true of man endowed with reason, might not the argument be expanded so as to include the Christian who has divine faith? If reason compels him to take up an instinctive attitude to the universe and life, is not faith itself a new vision of things and of human action? Either faith means a new outlook and a vision of the universe and life, or it means nothing at all. It is only by a mental outlook first of all that life can be transformed. Ideas are so necessary to life that without them action is not strictly human, and whatever else the Christian Faith may be (we know it includes divine condescension and good will on the part of man), it is a mental fact that must express itself in ideas about things and in a vision of life. St. Thomas very tersely described faith as the beginning of vision, having in mind the destiny of men which faith reveals, and Catholic theologians have always been inspired by St. Paul's account of it as revealing to the human mind a new world, the substance of things to come.

If the natural man, as we have argued, is called upon to render conscious his unconscious philosophy, does not the same logic compel us to say that the Christian, whose mind is endowed with faith, must also rationalize, as far as possible, his outlook? Rationalize is not perhaps the best word since faith, though intellectual, can never be fully expressed in terms of human reason. But a Christian starting from his faith is obliged by the logic of our argument to articulate his faith, to develop its content, and avail of its suggestions to meet the universe and life. The Christian faith does undoubtedly purport to give a man an all-embracing outlook on the world. How can this outlook in all its far-reaching significance be rendered conscious, how can it be enlarged so as to light up all Christian experience if not by means of a philosophy? If faith is an outlook, then it must contain an implicit philosophy, and the Christian cannot escape the task of unfolding the philosophy of his faith.

To this way of viewing philosophy and faith an objection may be urged. Philosophy by its nature is the outcome of the natural activity of the human mind; it does not take account of revelation on the part of God. Faith, on the other hand, is an account of things accepted not on the basis of reason only, but on the authority of God. Are not faith and philosophy then opposed? By accepting faith as a vision of the universe and life, has not the Christian surrendered the claims of natural reason? Reason has its own world to investigate, a world that is naturally accessible to the human mind, a world which is the proper object of human intelligence and ruled by its own natural laws. But faith accepts a new universe, and bases the existence of this new world not on reason but on authority.

This objection may look crude, but it is no more baldly stated than it is conceived by many minds. There are people who, accepting some form of belief, give one the impression that for them the only escape is to let life alternate between faith and reason, between belief and philosophy, and by keeping them apart save their belief from the scorching light of reason. "I have, ever since I was an undergraduate," wrote the late Dr. Gore, "been certain that I must be in the true sense a free thinker, and that either not to think freely about a disturbing subject, or to accept ecclesiastical authority in place of the best judgment of my own reason, would be for me an impossible treason against the light."[1] In line with this it comes natural to Dr. Gore to suggest that others, unlike himself, in desire for religious peace "take refuge under the shelter of some religious authority which admits of no questioning, whether it be the Roman Catholic Church or Christian Science."[2]

I have no brief for Christian Science, but it was news to hear from Dr. Gore that those who accept ecclesiastical authority do so "in spite of the best judgment of their reason." As for "taking shelter," the Church is largely hospitable in her assurance of the truth, but it is as the

---

[1] *Belief in God*, p. x.
[2] *Ibid.*, p. i.

*true* Church that she advertises herself to unbelievers. To accept the truth there must be reasons, and the Church invites no allegiance that is not reasonable. There are times when it is reasonable not to question. One of these is when Truth itself speaks and when we have reasons to believe that Truth has spoken.

One would have thought that the Church had lived down such calumnies as stare at one from the words of Dr. Gore. The distinction between faith and reason is a very old one. In the writings of Aquinas it was so clearly marked that the same mind could not be said to have faith and reason in a particular object from exactly the same point of view: if a man really *knew* a particular object he could not merely *believe* in it. But this distinction, as Aquinas showed, is not one of opposition, for the simple reason that truth cannot conflict with truth. In the last resort, both faith and reason have come from God, and God *is* Truth.

As for this alternating, departmental view of faith and reason, of belief and philosophy, Aquinas fought it to the end when he set out to refute what is known as the doctrine of a twofold truth. According to this pernicious theory a thing might be true for reason and not for faith or vice versa, and so reason and faith were radically opposed. Truth is one, replied St. Thomas. God is Truth and Truth itself is God. Intelligence is the faculty of truth, and what the human mind sees to be impossible is impossible for God and man. In view of that it was impossible to contemplate a clash between any established truth of reason and a truth of faith. So confident was he in philosophy that if anything, said he, is to be found contrary to faith in the writings of the philosophers, that is due not to the use, but to the abuse of philosophy.

No thinker can for long lead a double life, or put off his reasoning faculty on the plea that he wishes rather to believe. The idea of faith implied in this is an erroneous one; it looks upon faith as some form of confidence (*fiducia*) or feeling that is liable to be scorched out of existence by the rays of light. For why should one stifle his intelligence in defense of faith, if it isn't that he has a wrong idea of faith or that he fears that reason will put forward difficulties that will endanger faith? In this matter the Catholic is a realist, he knows that it is the very nature of mind to enquire, and the only limit that is set is one dictated by common prudence. "For I say, by the grace that is given me, to all that are among you, not to be more wise than it behoveth to be wise, but to be wise unto sobriety."[3] St. Paul counseled prudence no less than the Apostle Peter exhorted Christians to be "ready always to satisfy everyone that asketh you a reason of that hope which is in you."[4]

Reason is an approach to faith. No one believes unless it is reasonable to believe. But faith, once evoked because of its real motive, that of God's revealing, introduces the Christian to a God more clearly grasped than it is possible for reason to know, a Triune God, and lights up a larger universe, revealing depths in human life that unaided reason could never discern. But the effect of this revelation is not to destroy reason. Faith simply indicates the way that must be trodden. The subjective effect of the illumination of faith on the human mind is not to dis-

[3] Rom. 12:3.
[4] I Pet. 3:15.

pense reason from activity and from philosophic inquiry. When the road is indicated one must walk along it; and if faith is present the human mind is still the instrument of its own research and thinking. The nature of the Christian's mind, in a word, remains unchanged; but having faith it simply works under new conditions. The Christian who has faith is still able to philosophize rationally, he must tackle philosophic problems, the nature of his instrument of research remains unaltered, but having faith the exercise of his reason is facilitated considerably. In one case the mind has a torch of light which serves as a guide; in the other, where faith is not present, the human mind proceeds without a guide. In either case, guide or no guide, the human mind must traverse the journey. The Christian philosopher, as a philosopher, does not base his reasonings or conclusions on faith: he bases them on natural principles.

St. Thomas epitomized the relations of reason and faith in a single phrase: grace does not destroy, but perfects nature. Back of this synoptic account he possessed a large vision of the universe as a hierarchy of orders where one order of things or level depended on that immediately above it for its perfection. To illustrate this we have only to think of the physical universe in regard to the human mind. It is certain that the universe has meaning. That meaning, as far as the universe itself is concerned, is only potential. It is man who expresses the meaning of the physical universe: he stoops to confer upon it the perfection of meaning which is hidden from itself.

But man, he points out, is so made, with intelligence and will, that he is somehow immediately within the empire of God's influence. Why could not God then stoop to give to man a knowledge, a revelation, which man of himself could never achieve? By accepting this knowledge in faith man is in a position to see more deeply into the universe and to read the secret of God's destiny for his life. In keeping with this view of Aquinas is that grandiose vision of all science which Lacordaire in a celebrated passage has left us. "Science," says Lacordaire, "is the conjunction of the relations which constitute and bind all creation, from God down to the atom, from the infinitely small up to the infinitely great. Each step, in following up this vast ladder, illumines the step which precedes it and the one which follows, because each comprehended relation, in whatever mode this comprehension is effected, from below to above, or vice versa, is a revelation of that which is. Or in other words, the effect manifests the cause, because it is an image of it; the cause explains the effect, because it is the beginning of the first. Nevertheless this reciprocity is not equal, because, while the True Light descends from above, here below we have only a simple reflection. 'We see now through a glass in a dark manner,' says St. Paul, 'but then face to face' (1 Cor. 13). Philosophy in its present state therefore is necessarily imperfect, because we do not see face to face the starting-point and end — God. However much it may be manifested to our sight, it is not possible to know it but by the reflection which is contained in inferior things. Before God appeared He revealed His name. The voluntary acceptation of this Sovereign Word is called faith. Faith makes the Christian. When the Christian is in the possession of this new element of knowledge, from this point of view of the Highest he can descend even to the extreme ends of the universe, interpret from the relations which constitute the divine Essence, those relations which constitute the essence of man and of nature; after this, by the help of a *converse* movement, he verifies, by the laws which govern finite beings, the laws of the Infinite Being. This comparison of the two worlds — the illumination of the second, which is the effect, by the first, which is the cause, and the verification of the first, which is the cause, by the second, which is the effect: this flux and reflux of light, this current, which goes from the ocean toward the stream: faith in science and science in faith — this constitutes the Christian philosopher."

In this account, which is inspiring as a map of the universe of knowledge, Lacordaire does not distinguish between philosophy and theology. For him there is a certain continuity in all science, from theology, which takes dogmas as first principles, down to the sciences of matter that presuppose certain postulates. This outlook, so firmly grasping the wholeness of knowledge, is itself a philosophic one: it is strangely absent from the world of today. The age in which we live is strikingly departmental. By a necessary division of labor there are very many sciences, but few strive to keep the entire universe of knowledge before their minds. Our sense of the unity of things has grown dim; our vision of the universe, as affected by the Incarnation, and of life, as destined for a supernatural vision, has become blurred. If God became Man, as the Christian believes, and if the supernatural has been infused into the natural life of man, then the Incarnation and the supernatural destiny made possible by Redemption go to form the natural life of man in its integrity. The integral human order in which we live is one that has its source in the Incarnation and its destiny in a face-to-face vision of God. It is the mission of philosophy to keep alive man's consciousness of wholeness, to give him a sense of the integral order and unity of the universe and man. If this unity and order for the Christian is bound up with Christ, as for the natural man it is linked up with God, is not the Christian bound to articulate his vision, to light up the whole with the light that comes both from faith and reason?

In an effort to accomplish this task of unfolding the content of his faith by reason, where will the Christian turn for help? The philosophies of the hour are particularly uninspiring; they lack the very thing that gives philosophy value. Philosophy is a sense of unity, but the philosophies of the moment are almost as numerous as philosophers themselves, they are the outcome of particular attitudes. Further, the fact that these philosophies are the outcome of so many different attitudes, scientific or economic or social and political, indicates that no real attempt is made to comprise the whole of life. It is not that the problems dealt with by modern philosophers are not important, but that the spirit in which they are treated is not broad or philosophic enough. "Man must know what to do and how to act," it has been said, "but he craves yet more the knowledge of who he is, and why he is here at all, and what he is here for."[5]

There is only one factor on last analysis which can unify human life. Religion alone can bind together the energies of life, for if life is intelligible only when related to God, then it is to religion as the bond of man and God that we must go for inspiration. Where, then, shall we seek for a philosophy of life that is religious in inspiration if

---

[5]Randall, G. H., *The Spirit of the New Philosophy*, p. 41.

not in an epoch when the sense of the unity of things was more firmly grasped than it is at the present day? Admittedly that epoch in the history of human thought and institutions was the medieval era, which presents an example of a culture that was fully orbed and complete. Medieval culture achieved a unification of its forces that is striking. On the external side Europe was one in a way that it never has been since. On the inner side the various aspects of its culture took root in a single spirit. The soul of medieval culture that expressed itself effectively in its philosophy of life was religion. "Religion in fact," writes Mr. J. MacMurray, "is that aspect of culture which alone can unify the human spirit, either in the individual or as a society of men. It is the absence of religion in the modern world that makes it impossible to achieve a human unity, for the external unity of a civilization can only be the outward expression of the inner unity of the spirit. It is this religious unity of culture which the medieval world achieved that we usually refer to as Christianity."[6]

The Christianity of the Middle Ages found an intellectual expression in the philosophy of St. Thomas Aquinas that has riveted the attention of our contemporaries. One of the striking and hopeful features of the contemporary mind is its interest in St. Thomas. His centenary a few years ago was in many respects significant. By a remarkable coincidence that year also marked the centenary of Immanuel Kant, and the clash which Eucken in 1901 declared to be one of two entirely distinct worlds seemed nonexistent: those who came to celebrate Kant spoke warmly of the great Aquinas. But the striking fea-

---

[6]*Some Makers of the Modern Spirit*, ed. by J. MacMurray, p. 5.

ture of the system of St. Thomas is the fundamental unity
that he wrought, not only in his person by a wedding of
philosophy and sanctity, but in his whole system. His
doctrine is one of the most impressive forms of intellectualism ever framed, it breathes a trust and confidence in
the human intellect never surpassed, and yet, by no mere
accident, but by a law of his very intellectuality, the system
of Aquinas is inspiringly religious in character. For while
a first acquaintance with his system inspires one with his
imperturbable confidence in intelligence and his absolute
contempt in philosophic matters for irrational elements,
yet one rises from his system with the impression that he
makes no exorbitant claims for the *human* form of intelligence and reason. "The really decisive factor for intelligence is infallible truth, and every time it allows itself
to be carried away by a testimony that could deceive there
is disorder." But if intelligence is the faculty of the real
whose object is wide and limitless being, its position in the
scale of things must determine the greatness and relative
limitations of its grasp. Identical with being in God, the
divine intelligence sees the whole of everything in an intuition of God's own essence. But this cannot be said of
angel or of man. The angel knows, too, by intuition of its
essence things that belong to its natural and finite world.
But man is least of all in the order of intelligences: "The
soul of man is the last of the series of beings endowed
with intelligence and of all man possesses the least share
of intellectual capacity." Man must supply for lack of intuition by the laborious process of reasoning and thinking.

But in this tremendous effort, whereby man supplies
for vital intuition by discursive reasoning, there is implicit
in man's outlook a hope and a demand. St. Thomas does

not go the lengths of modern idealistic thinkers for whom
the world is rational through and through, for whom a
single fact becomes what the crystal is to the magician —
"the ball that images the world," and for whom the irrational surd of matter and contingencies of time and space
have entirely disappeared. He does not give us an apothe-
osis of the human mind nor would he accept the ideal of
unwitting Tennyson:

> Little flower — but if I could understand
> What you are, root and all, and all in all,
> I should know what God and man is.

The hope and demand that St. Thomas recognizes in
all human efforts to know is simply that there must exist
an ultimate perspective for which all things are intelligible. Many things surpass the mind of man, but absolutely speaking there is nothing which is not somewhere
understood. There exists, he says, a form of intellectual
activity which is infinite in its efficacy and which we call
God.

The human mind then, in its conquest of reality, must
affirm at every step implicitly the existence of God as sole
explaining Cause of all, and if to explain the universe, a
contingent world where matter plays the role of the irrational and where the concrete individual remains "in-
effable," man must at every moment appeal to God, yet
the human intellect must resign itself to silence where
the inner life and mystery of God's own nature is concerned. True, the capacities of the human mind are great,
they have for object being, which in itself is illimited and
indefinite, and no matter what conquest it may make by
its own unaided powers, there will be in the human in-

tellect a residual capacity that is unexhausted. But it was precisely in this wondrous capacity that St. Thomas saw the greatness of man's intelligence. Precisely because no finite object could fill up the mind of man, and because of itself by its own unaided powers it could not exhaust its own capacities, St. Thomas said that the human intellect was *capax Dei;* it could be worked upon by God, and in obedience to divine power could be made to see what natively it could not see. On the threshold of the divine then St. Thomas placed the human mind in its proper posture, worshiping the mystery of the Godhead but ready to accept whatever increment of perfection God might be willing to bestow. It was absolutely impossible for a finite mind to know what these designs of God might be. But did God reveal His intentions for humanity, as Aquinas believed He did, then the human mind would be found open in its wide capacities for the message that would come to it from God. It was the greatness of his intellectualism that it recognized the inherent incapacity of philosophy to exhaust itself. For philosophy, as the output of human reason, must share in the impotency of reason. At the highest peak of its ascent the human mind must avow to itself that God is mystery and that it cannot exhaust its own capacities. Aquinas saw that the human mind was never more itself than when it surpassed itself in this avowal, and when he showed that the new light that comes in faith does not destroy the human reason but enhances it, making it to remain itself when it has surpassed the reach of its native powers, he might well claim that his philosophy was religious, not in spite of his intellectualism, but precisely because of it. In this union of philosophy and religion lies the hope for an era that is hopelessly divided since the Renaissance, when man became the center of things and lost the only perspective in which civilization and culture can go hand in hand.

The modern progress in civilization has not brought with it a corresponding increase of culture. Civilization is interested rather in the external conditions of man's life than in the quality of his life, whether individual or social. If the philosopher is not to succumb to the disease that it is his office to diagnose, he must call in the aid of religion. It is not enough to *know,* even when one's knowledge is as universal as philosophy; men must *live,* and their lives must be full-orbed and cultured. Without religion which commands the whole of man in his personal and social character there can be no unified or lasting culture; philosophy as an element of culture must itself feel the breath of religious inspiration. The task of philosophy, then, is less exalted than that of religion, which must knit together all man's powers.

In an age, however, when the medieval unity of religion has been apparently dissolved forever, the immediate and pressing need is one that affects the philosopher. If the structure of human life is to be held together even by the force of religion it must first take root in human soil; it is essential to dig anew the foundations of human sanity. Before a man can live a human life he must be convinced that a human life is worth living. Under the medieval conditions of culture it was unthinkable that any number of men should need convincing; for them the question simply did not arise. But it is otherwise today. In endeavoring to answer the question, Is Life Worth Living?, we are undertaking a very necessary spade-work before the divine Artisan and His human co-worker can begin to raise up in time that temple of eternity, man. For if life is not worth while, if skepticism has so poisoned the wells of human nature that life appears to signify a radically "thwarted purposing," if

> Crass Casualty obstructs sun and rain
> And dicing Time for gladness casts a moan . . .

then the unhappy individual so convinced can merely encumber the earth with worthless living until he is swept into a grave of deep oblivion. It is the purpose of this book to combat such insanity and to show that life has meaning, that life is something of such high and broad dimensions that the universe is too small and narrow to contain it and that time itself is far too meager a meal to satisfy its hunger.

# 7

# Is Life Worth Living?

It will facilitate matters for the reader if I may suggest the approach we are about to make to what is the central problem for discussion. It will be my endeavor to show in this chapter why the question, *Is Life Worth Living?*, is no mere academic dispute, but a very vital problem that is engaging the minds of our contemporaries in almost every domain of investigation, and why it is invested almost with tragic interest for the epoch in which we live above all the other centuries that have lost themselves in the tide of time. In the next chapter I hope to give conclusive proofs to show that human life, whether as mere existence and duration, or as human life proper in its growth and enrichment of itself by contact with a reality other than itself, is of incalculable intrinsic value and of such significance and import that time is not enough to exhaust its meaning. In subsequent chapters an effort will be made to outline the ancient and modern views of life and to indicate what alone makes the life of men worth while. One dare not hope, of course, to exhaust a detailed

account of what makes life worth living for the individual, since for every man there exists inevitably a margin
of freedom and of choice. But it will be possible to rule
out the supposedly essential obstacles that may threaten
the value of human life and to state convincingly the essential thing that will rescue human life from the abyss
of sheer futility so well expressed by Shakespeare:

> To-morrow, and to-morrow, and to-morrow,
> Creeps in this petty pace from day to day,
> To the last syllable of recorded Time;
> And all our yesterdays have lighted fools
> The way to dusty death. Out, out, brief candle!
> Life's but a walking shadow; a poor player,
> That struts and frets his hour upon the stage,
> And then is heard no more: it is a Tale
> Told by an idiot, full of sound and fury,
> Signifying nothing.

This essential thing to life is religion. Life without religion is life without meaning,

>            . . . a Tale
> Told by an idiot, full of sound and fury,
> Signifying nothing.

By then the Christian anxious to think things out for
himself under the inspiration of his Faith will be in a
position to assess at its true value the contribution to the
problem of life made by his Master, Christ. Philosophy
will serve to enhance the imperative necessity of the only
religion that is true, the religion of Him whom Christians
accept as God's own solution for life's enigma, the Man-
God, Jesus Christ.

The acknowledgment of God in Christ,
Accepted by thy reason, solves for thee
All questions in the earth and out of it,
And has so far advanced thee to be wise.

Should the reader have come to the consideration of this problem of life's value with no feeling that it is a question of real live or pressing interest, it is necessary to disillusion him. "A great change is working through our Western civilization," writes Mr. Alfred Noyes in his recent book, *The Unknown God,* "and none can foresee the outcome. There are vast forces moving, not upon the face of the deep, but below the surface, out of sight; and neither men nor nations can tell whither we are drifting. 'Drifting' is the word, for an ultimate goal and purpose in our lives are no longer believed to be discernible by the human intellect. The task of keeping afloat a partially wrecked hulk so closely engages a greater part of the population that we have come to look upon the steering-gear as a relic of a superstitious age. There have been periods in which signs less vivid, though of precisely the same character, have announced that a civilization was dying. Even among the lights and music of the modern cities there must be few who are not sometimes haunted by the feeling that Belshazzar is once more the ruler of the feast; and certainly no thoughtful mind can lightly dismiss the many ominous indications that the long-prophesied 'Decline of the West' has already begun."

It is not merely that the goal and purpose of life are not discernible by the human intellect; but that men are now voicing the problem of life as a query. The very wording of the problem, *Is Life Worth Living?,* is distinctively new, of our own time. It was only yesterday, in the nineteenth century, that the eternal problem of human life assumed for men this distinctive guise of a query, and that for the first time in the history of human thought it was formulated in precisely these terms. May we not discern in this simple fact a world of meaning and significance?

That before this century there were inquiries into the meaning and purpose of human life I should be the last to deny. At all times men have been interested in the "why" of life; a volume might be filled with the sayings of men of every age and clime, wise and unwise, on human life. But the point that must be grasped is that an inquiry into the "why" of life is quite distinct from the problem, *Is Life Worth Living?* They are miles apart, from a certain point of view, and historically there is a gulf of centuries between them.

It is perfectly clear, for instance, that, in the thirteenth century, the great thinker, Aquinas, indicated a goal of human life and put forward a philosophy of life in which were summed up the teachings both of Greek philosophy and of Christian Patrology. It is likewise certain that, in the sixteenth century, Lord Francis Bacon made himself the spokesman of an entirely new ideal of life, the modern view, which admittedly differs in many respects from the more ancient view of Aquinas and Aristotle. It matters little for our present purpose what these two views, the ancient and the modern, make of human life. What I want to emphasize is a certain implication common to both which marks them off very sharply from more recent investigations. When we have grasped the drift of the older inquiries and compared them with the contemporary outlook on life, we shall be in a position to see that there are three fundamental moments in the history of human conceptions of life, roughly corresponding to ancient, modern, and contemporary; and that, in the present state of knowledge, the contemporary attitude suggests a final stage beyond which it seems impossible to go.

It will not long escape the observant, that in the ancient and the modern views of life there is a common postulate and assumption. To outline a goal of life presupposes that life has a goal to be indicated. The preoccupations of Aquinas and Bacon with human life, differing as they do in the results of their inquiries, have this in common, that they arise out of the presumption, which they would not dream of questioning, that human life is a thing of value and endowed with meaning. Likewise, to seek out the "why" of life is tacitly to presuppose that life *has* a "why" and purpose, and to the philosophic mind of Aquinas that immediately is tantamount to admitting that human life is not its own sole sufficient reason, but that it is intelligible only when we take account of a Being beyond it. However that may be, it is easy to see that the contemporary approach to the problem of human life is quite new and distinctive, and marks an epoch in human inquiry. For instead of taking for granted the assumption in which the ancient and the modern views were rooted, the contemporary interest centers around this very assumption itself; it questions the very postulate of the purposiveness of human life. In this new approach the mind of our contemporaries is expressing the utter self-consciousness of our age, and it is as far removed from the outlook of the ancient and medievalist as modern skepticism in regard to the existence of an external world is alien to the dogmatic realism of a Doctor Johnson, who refuted all idealists by kicking a stone with his foot.

W. H. Mallock was in all probability the first to reach the reading public with this new and entirely actual outlook on human life. He published a book, entitled *Is Life Worth Living?,* in the second half of the nineteenth century.[1] That he was conscious of the novelty of his theme is clearly insinuated in his opening words: "What I am about to deal with in this book is a question which may well strike many, at first sight, as a question that has no serious meaning, or none at any rate for the sane and healthy mind. I am about to attempt inquiring, not sentimentally, but with all calmness and sobriety, into the true value of this human life of ours, as tried by those tests of reality which the modern world is accepting, and to ask dispassionately if it be worth the living. The inquiry has certainly been made before; but it has never been made properly, it has never been made in the true scientific spirit."[2] Another book, by the same writer, entitled *The New Republic,*[3] gives us a discussion of the same topic by a number of celebrated personages of his day.[4] The temper of the discussions may be caught from the following words addressed to the Catholic Lady of the piece, one Miss Cherton: "Your religion," says one to her, "is a kind of philosopher's stone, turning whatever it touches into something precious. But we — we can only remember that for us, too, things had a meaning once but they have it no longer. Life stares at us, now all bleak and

---

[1] *Is Life Worth Living?* New York, 1879.

[2] *Op. cit.*

[3] *The New Republic,* London, 1889.

[4] *The New Republic* may have been published before *Is Life Worth Living?* as he is given there as author of *The New Republic*. A third book of his is entitled *Atheism and the Value of Life* (London, 1884).

expressionless, like the eyes of a lost friend who is not dead but turned into an idiot. Perhaps you never read Clough's poems, did you? Scarcely a day passes in which I do not echo myself his words:

> A well-a-day, for we are souls bereaved,
> Of all the creatures under heaven's wide cope,
> We are the most hopeless who once had most hope,
> And most beliefless who had once believed."

The spirit of the nineteenth century is distinctly conveyed in these two quotations from Mallock, the first pointing to Mallock's conscious effort to prove the intrinsic worth of life, the second indicating the loss of worth and value brought about by disappearing faith and hope, by evanescent religion.

More significant still, the question asked by Mallock finds a thousand echoes in the literature of this epoch. Poetry was written with the title, *Is Life Worth Living?*, and it is the hidden spring of much poetic inspiration. The two outstanding poems of the nineteenth century, in fact, two poems that reflect the philosophy of the period, *Bishop Blougram's Apology*, by Browning, and Tennyson's *In Memoriam*, bear testimony to a common preoccupation, differently voiced, with the value of human life. Browning seems to bludgeon the enemies of faith in life with the club of triumphant optimism:

> From the first, Power was — I knew.
>   Life has made clear to me
> That, strive but for closer view,
>   Love were as plain to see.

For what greater proof of life's intrinsic value than a theory that the essence of existence is love, and this view of Browning was not the result of poetic sentiment alone, or religious intoxication, but a theory examined at the bar of reasoning. For Browning differs from most other poets in that he has endeavored to give a complete and reasoned view of man and of his relation to the world, a philosophy of life, in fact.

> The common problem, yours, mine, everyone's,
> Is not to fancy what more fair in life
> Provided it could be, but, finding first
> What may be, then find how to make it fair
> Up to our means — a very different thing!

And while in an effort of sympathy with his disputant, Mr. Gigadibs enters into the common spirit of unbelief, or tries to, he finds

> that belief,
> As unbelief before, shakes us by fits,
> Confounds us like its predecessor. . . .

for when one feels secure in unbelief, there is something to disturb security:

> Just when we are safest, there's a sunset-touch,
> A fancy from a flower-bell, someone's death,
> A chorus-ending from Euripides,—
> And that's enough for fifty hopes and fears,
> As old and new at once as nature's self,
> To rap and knock and enter in our soul,
> Take hands and dance there, a fantastic ring,
> Round the ancient idol, on his base again,—
> The grand Perhaps! We look on helplessly.
> There the old misgivings, crooked questions are.[5]

---

[5]*Bishop Blougram's Apology.*

So proceeds Bishop Blougram on his course:

> Belief or unbelief
> Bears upon life, determines its whole course,
> Begins at the beginning . . .
> 'Tis clear I cannot lead my life, at least
> Induce the world to let me peaceably,
> Without declaring at the outset, "Friends,
> I absolutely and peremptorily
> Believe" — I say, faith is my waking life.

This militant optimism of Browning will not be found in Tennyson, but a wish to believe, a wistful hope in the ultimate goodness of life, is present even when he seems to succumb to the atmosphere around him, as when he says:

> I often grew
> Tired of so much within our little life,
> Or of so little in our little life —
> Poor little life that toddles half an hour
> Crowned with a flower or two, and there an end.

But in this Tennyson is the perfect mirror of his epoch: he reflects the waning light that plays on life until his successor, George Eliot, will draw the blinds on life that shut out the light of God. For while Tennyson tried to hold fast to his vision, even through the material universe, of

> Some far-off divine event
> To which the whole creation moves,

George Eliot is confident that no such vision exists:

> Human time
> Shall fold its eyelids, and the human sky
> Be gathered like a scroll within the tomb
> Unread forever.

With Tennyson, then, there is still hope and trust

> That nothing walks with aimless feet;
> That not one life shall be destroyed,
> Or cast as rubbish to the void,
> When God hath made the pile complete.

That is his protest, a faint echo of Browning's optimism, against something in their era which was a menace to human sanity, something that seemed to dwarf the life of man.

> O life as futile, then, as frail!

These two poems of Browning and Tennyson I have selected as typical. What I want you to notice is that they together present a common front against a common enemy which seems to suggest the utter vanity and futility of human life. To them you can add the oft-quoted lines of Matthew Arnold, less buoyant than Browning, more critical than Tennyson, more perilously near the chasm of futility as he hears the tide of belief ebbing away from a desolate shore —

> But now I only hear
> Its melancholy, long withdrawing roar,
> Retreating, to the breath
> Of the night-wind, down the vast edges drear
> And naked shingles of the world.

They are all protesting, each in his own way, for a conception of life that is being threatened in their time. Now, what is the common enemy they are fighting? On the surface it is waning belief, that reaches its climax in George Eliot who dogmatizes in negation. But what is the new thing that seems to bring in its wake this unbelief? It is, in a word, the scientific conception of life so dominant in the nineteenth century, so dogmatic before 1870.

For what, in a word, was the scientific view of life as indicated by the triumphant success of science in the first half of this century?

The scientific conception of life in the nineteenth century was a particular aspect of a wider outlook on the universe at large. At this time, the scientists hoped to light up the world, to disclose its mysteries, and reveal it in the stark nakedness of matter subject to motion and its laws. Science was really attempting to be a philosophy and to give a complete account of all reality by aid of the purely mechanical concept of quantity. In such a system, the first tenet was the rigid determinism of all the world's happenings, with no regard to purpose or finality. But if all things were ultimately reducible to matter it followed, secondly, that man was merely body. Materialism denied the existence of soul and spirit as something distinct from body or capable of surviving it: everything in man, to his highest-soaring thought or noblest spiritual emotion, was simply the phosphorescence of his brain. The soul was born with the body, grew with it, and with extinction of life the soul was dead. Add to these two principles the hypothesis of evolution in its first crudity, applied not only to man but to human history, and you have a picture of human life evolved after countless ages from matter of which all things are made, and of human theories as the unfolding of mere human opinions which, in the case of religion, claimed to have been of heavenly origin and Godly revelation. So large had become the ambition of physical science before 1870 that it took the world for its province, and its effort to explain all things forms an epoch in its history.

What a Tennyson and many another poet saw was the disturbing character of this world-view of science, its stark incompetency even in matters physical where quality stood for something, and its peculiarly uninspiring account of human life. For if the world is a universe without aim or purpose, an accidental happening, the origins of which were nebulous and the working out of which is purposeless, then nothing seems worth while, since a world without purpose is a world without values. The sacrosanct character of the human spirit, hitherto accepted as privileged, was torn into shreds, and man himself stood revealed as an accidental appearance on the surface of an aimless whirling cosmos.

In time, of course, the scientists were to learn that the scientific approach to life was only one of many and the least satisfying of all. For the human spirit possesses other functions which are no less vital and no less profound; nor can they be explained away out of existence by the categories of natural science. Art, for instance, has never been reduced to science; nor has poetry. Moral life, with its insistence on freedom, is irreducible to scientific concepts. But in a theory of life all these data, irreducible as they are, must be taken into account. The scientist of today, we may say, is humbly penitent and modest in his claims. But even in the best examples of repentance we cannot help noticing a kind of stubborn emphasis, inherited, no doubt, upon the littleness of mere man as compared with the thundering greatness of the cosmic worlds with which the scientist is acquainted. Even today there is an atmosphere about scientific accounts of life which inclines one to stoop abashed before the greatness of massed material forces. But in this there is nothing less than a phobia of cosmic greatness, signs of which are not absent from the best accredited popular exponents of scientific theories. Witness the final words with which Sir James Jeans closes his best-seller.

Give a false idea a start, however, and you will never catch up on it until it has gone the round of popular magazines, found its way into the unconscious minds of men and women, and perhaps ended by marching a man to death or destruction. There is something fatal about the suggestiveness of wrong ideas. I remember reading an account of a hysterical young lady who was reading a novel in which the heroine, she imagined, was strikingly like herself. As the plot thickened, this young lady became more and more like her heroine . . . and when the heroine ended by committing suicide, the young lady had an irresistible impulse to do the same . . . and did it. The scientific view of life, now abandoned by scientists of the first rank, is still going its rounds, eating its way into many human hopes, and corroding human lives. As if to perpetuate the menace, a type of literature, styled Realism, glories in its gospel of life's futility. And Realism, Emile Zola once said, is simply the scientific method applied to life. Now I am not decrying simply the hold on facts that realist literature claims to have, for all human art, limited in its creativeness, must live on facts. But I would indict that Realism which is not only the application of scientific method in its best sense but of that pseudo-scientific theory of the nineteenth century which condemns life to utter and irretrievable futility. That this distrust of life is the gospel of many Realists is something undeniable. For on the "plea of facing facts of modern life," they would condemn all forms of romanticism that assert the plasticity of life, the triumph of ideals, or the unconquerable spirit of human life. To speak of such things, say they, is a self-delusion that is blind to the gaunt and haggard form of the reality of human life. Take, for example, the works of Charles Dickens as contrasted with the writings of George Moore or Aldous Huxley. Dickens had reason to know the realities of life. As a youth, it has been said of him that he was "dragged through a drain-pipe by the ears,"[6] and from a neglected waifdom in the streets, from work among foul associates in a blacking-factory, and from the horrors and hypocrisies of a debtors' prison, he emerged to affirm the inherent goodness of human life, to influence his age, to liberate the school from Squeers, the hospital from Sarah Gamp. Dickens, in fact, was a reformer because "of his faith in life, of life's value, and of life's plasticity under the influence of ideas. To read Dickens is to feel the impulse to improve life," life is worth modifying; to read George Moore or Huxley one feels that life is not worth changing, even if it could be reformed, and it is hard to see how it can be reformed since it is in the grip of some blind fatality. Even Thomas Hardy's finest book, *Tess of D'Urbervilles,* is vitiated by Hardy's own gospel of life's futility. "Tess of D'Urbervilles," it has been said, "is a pure song of the triumph of life and goodness as far, at least, as the death of Alec D'Urberville, whose murderer, by the way, was never Tess Durbeyfield, but one Thomas Hardy, a propagandist

---

[6]Watts, N., "Poiêsis and the Modern World," *Dublin Review,* October, 1933, p. 252.

fiction-writer." Of course an author may do what he will with his own, nor do I think that writers are bound to finish up their novels always with happy endings, or even see the triumph of good on this side of the grave, but I cite Realism advisedly as the gospel of life's futility, for in many of its writers it goes the full length of crushing life beneath the hard heel of a blind fatality. Granting that literature holds the mirror up to life, in the literature of our epoch we can discern the forms of the very many — legion is their name — in that unhappy paradox of living and not believing that life is worth the candle.

An excellent example of one at grips with this accepted futility of human life is to be had in the intimate journal of one Mlle. Bashkirtself, cited by Birrell in his *Men, Women and Books.*[7] "What is there in us," she asks, "that, in spite of plausible arguments — in spite of the consciousness that all leads to nothing — one should still grumble. I know that, like everyone else, I am going on towards death and nothingness. I weigh the circumstances of life and, whatever they may be, they appear to me miserably vain, and, for all that, I cannot resign myself. Then it must be a force; it must be a *something* — not merely a 'passage,' a certain period of time which matters little whether it is spent in a palace or a cellar; there is something stronger, truer, than our foolish phrases about it all. It is life, in short; not merely a passage — an unprofitable misery — but life that we hold most dear, all that we call ours, in short. People say it is nothing because we do not possess eternity. Ah! the fools. Life is ourselves, it is ours, it is all that we possess; how then is it possible to say it is nothing? If this is *nothing* then show me something."

[7]Cheap edition, p. 45.

Here we have an example of clinging on, an effort to hold to life which appeals to our pity because of the very slender grip it manifests to reason. But this desperate situation, not unlike an Alpine climber poised in mid-air and depending for life on a grip of a withering patch of green on a bare rock, is a stage toward the paradox of our time which suggests that the only meaning to be discovered in life is that life has no meaning, and which sends so many individuals to quaff life's essence avariciously from all life's pools. "We know that life is short and we must all die," says H. G. Wells in one of his wise moments, "and the greater multitude of us is driven by that thought to an incessant pursuit of small distractions. . . . The individual is confronted, but not plainly and frankly, with a need for re-making himself, and this task appears more monstrous than it really is. So he wavers continually in his conduct and his judgments. *He complains of a disorder and futility in life that is indeed only in himself.*" But the ranks of such deluded individuals, we fear, are crowded. "Doubt of *life* — of the act of living — is more widespread than the more fortunate people think. It is not that some of them doubt God or revelation: they have not reached such considerations. Disgust begins long before that. You will find that this is not only in 'bohemian' or absinthe-minded quarters, but in students' clubs, as well as more workaday quarters; and the results are discernible sometimes in conduct and in open tragedy — most often in mentality."[8]

---

[8]Blyton, W. J., *The Modern Adventure*, p. 25.

# 8

# The Value of Life

"Those who believe that pessimism had its rise in Germany in the nineteenth century are blind and forgetful."[1] Papini, who wrote these lines, will have it that most of the "reports on mankind," books like the *Odyssey*, the *Divine Comedy, Don Quixote, Faust*, contain reviews of human life that are sad and bitter; and in the writings of Dean Swift of the eighteenth century he finds "the most definitive condemnation of life as we live it."[2] There is a difference, however, between those accounts of human life which content themselves with emphasizing the tragicomedy of life as men actually live it and an indictment of life in virtue of abstract principles. There is a sense, in fact, in which optimism or pessimism cannot be properly discussed until we have fixed on fundamental principles. Normally, one is not in a position to judge of actual life in favor of optimism or pessimism for two reasons. If the question is to be decided by a summation of life's

---

[1]Papini, *Four and Twenty Minds*, p. 227.
[2]*Ibid.*

good things as compared with life's evil elements, then one should have too long to wait. Deeper still, an evaluation of life must depend upon a discovered standard of what constitutes good and evil for the life of man. The pessimism of Schopenhauer is an example of a condemnation of life on principle. For him the will-to-live was the root of all misery, and escape lies in the extinction of the human race.

The origin of a pessimistic outlook, then, may or may not be due to German philosophy, but sufficient has been said to show that the approach to the problem of human life suggested by the query, *Is Life Worth Living?*, is distinctive and significant. Before the nineteenth century it was customary to investigate the "why" and purpose of life; for our epoch it was reserved to broach the question, whether life had any real purpose or not. In its new form the problem ceases to be an academic dispute, it is invested with tragic interest for many and it induces a mood which threatens to become an accepted attitude.

It is necessary to react against such a mood, and the best kind of reaction is to be had in an intellectual fight for the value of life. No real thinker can sympathize for long with a doubt of life that is radical and final. I have not now in mind that scientific skepticism which both Aristotle and Aquinas declare to be the beginning of all wisdom. It is perfectly certain that one must look at problems long and hard before one can hope to solve them, and for that a kind of skepticism, which is knowledge conscious of its limitations, is an essential. But there is a difference between doubting well and dogmatizing in doubt. Skepticism is never so unconvincing as when it dogmatizes in negations. One may legitimately smile at the man who declares, with truth as he thinks, that there is no such thing as truth, and it is permissible to be at least suspicious of the man who, leasing life for as long a period as possible, announces with conviction that life is blank and futile. Frequently skepticism is simply a cloak for selfishness. There is a subtle form of it which will affirm nothing, deny nothing, in the hope of enjoying things indefinitely. Such a sophisticated form of skepticism is hampered by nothing, checked by nothing, it luxuriates in each passing mood, it would taste mystic joys or drink from the pools of pleasure. But skepticism of this kind is simply playing with life, endeavoring to trick it; it shirks primal certainties and pretends to a freedom which is license.

Skepticism in regard to the value of life will have one advantage if it succeeds in stabbing people into wakefulness. The value of life, its glory and possibilities, the extent of its reach and the far-flung horizons which it demands are frequently missed because of men's undisturbed acceptance of it. So many live from hand to mouth, passing their days from bed to breakfast, from home to office, from office to home . . . and so to bed, that they are unaware of the real inner story of life as the unfolding of deep desires, of human endeavors, of a heart throbbing in love and hatred, of a soul rich with capacities of feeling and emotion, of a spirit daring, which in its onward course would shatter rocks, turn back the tides of circumstance, and set out on uncharted seas: their sense of life is dimmed and, too accustomed to it, they miss the apocalypse of life within.

To illustrate the truth of this, take the experiment, once performed, with a pair of spectacles. This particular pair was so devised that the person who looked through them would see things inverted. At first the man who looked was dazed — naturally. But in precisely two seconds and a half he noticed that things were back again in position, as they were. The rapidity of this new adaptation of the human retina to a changed situation, making it appear the normal, is symptomatic of the force of habit: the strangest things seem ordinary and the constant miracle of existence is a thing of no undue importance.

Mr. G. K. Chesterton is always tilting at this common blindness of everyday life. If you wish to get the gist of his wise nonsense, recall to mind one of those inimitable stories of his. It is the history of a man who elopes with his own wife; who burgles his own safe; and wanders around the world to walk in at the front door of his own house. Mr. Chesterton is always threatening — to the constant amusement of his reader — to come back to this favorite theme, and write an epic on the man who sailed away from his native country in a fog to return and discover it as some forgotten island. The point he makes is that the husband of the story reminded himself that he was married by acting the part of the ardent lover and eloping with his wife; he assured himself that he was a proprietor by coveting his own safe's contents as if it belonged to a neighbor; he renewed his joy in home, like the explorer in the fog, by pretending to have discovered it for the first time.

The allegory perfectly fits the relation of men to life. All are wedded to life for good or ill; few really know the consort with whom they pass their days; many have discovered her value only just as they were about to part with her. "All science," says the same writer, "is a sublime detective story. Only it is not set to detect why a man is dead; but the darker secret of why we are alive at all." It is just the merit of the contemporary doubt of life that it may worry us into wakefulness and make us seek the darker secret of why we are alive.

To supply a convincing answer, we must distinguish in life the two aspects that are bound up with it. In the first place, we can consider life as pure existence and continued existence or duration, and see if from this viewpoint human life may be said to be worth while. If it is, then we can dig our feet in solidly to examine the second aspect of life which considers the environment of human life, the objects that are destined to enrich or impoverish it, the network of events and circumstances that surrounds it, the ultimate horizon that human life demands. Life is always a question of adaptation to environment: vitality and environment go together, mutually influencing one another. Is there anything in the complete and integral environment of human life that would seem to thwart it, or negative in any way the worth and value that accrues to it from the perfection of existence and duration? Is there any force that can break and shatter the aspiration that glows from the presence of a spirit in a human body? When these questions have been settled, we shall be in a position, not only to believe in the value of life, but we shall know. It will then be merely a question of what it is that makes a human life worth while.

When we start with the simple fact of existence and of life's duration, we are beginning at the beginning with a vengeance. But this starting point is not only useful and necessary in view of the skepticism which saps the very roots of existence by calling it in question, but also in view of everyday somnolence that does not wake up to ask the question at all. Philosophy is always asking questions, and that is why there is something of a child in every philosopher. A child could ask as many questions in five minutes as you or I could not answer in a lifetime. But the simplest fact, no matter what it is, is a note of interrogation with many facets. Every fact is a problem — first, a problem that it is at all; secondly, why it is; and thirdly, how it came about. No philosophy is complete that does not raise these three questions. Now, in regard to life, we may start with the fact of it. That we are alive, is a fact. We know it. "I think," said Descartes, "therefore I am." We may eliminate the *therefore*. The fact of our existence is given immediately. But if I am at all, then the next question ought to be why I am, why I am alive, and after that, how life made its appearance upon the earth. We may eliminate the third. Facts are facts, even when we don't know how they came about: of course we *do* know — but we are not interested in that now. But instead of going from the fact to ask the "why" of life, our contemporaries begin to heckle about the nature of the fact itself. That human life exists may as a fact be just an accident in a cosmic universe. But before going on to ask the "why" of that fact, they insist that we must first ask if it has any "why."

If human life is a fact, then it must have a *why:* every fact must have a sufficient reason for its existence. Even if life were an accidental appearance on the surface of an evolving universe, it must have an explanation, granting that its ultimate explanation may be obscure. Even accidents must have a reason for their occurrence, no matter how baffling their sudden appearance may be; accidents are not things that arrive from nowhere, or simply happen: they must have causes. For if a simple event or happening has no sufficient reason for its existence, then nothing has. Could a single fact escape this necessity of having a sufficient reason for its existence, then all facts can, and what is more, the sum of facts would be in the same position. The whole question centers in the little word "is": a single fact "is," the whole world of fact "is," but if one single fact needs no reason why it is, then the whole world of fact is also exempt from the same necessity. From this point of view there is nothing more in the world of fact than in a single fact: both "are." But to emancipate all reality from the necessity of explanation in this fashion is to empty it of meaning. Hence, either the simple fact of life has meaning, or nothing has. And if nothing has meaning there can be no knowledge or science at all. For a scientist, then, to dispute the "why" of life is to condemn himself out of his own mouth: he declares his science impossible.

If human life has meaning, it is necessarily worth while. Neglect for the moment the final issues of man's life, his ultimate success or failure, and it must be admitted that existence is a perfection. The moment human life exists upon the face of the earth, there is an added perfection in the world: it is better to be than not to be, to have than not to have. This, in fact, is the dumb assertion of all creation: the stones of the way cry out against destruction; living things are self-assertive and struggle for life; in man the will-to-live is the voice of life itself, imperiously demanding continued life. Precisely because this instinct for life is so deep in man, issuing out from the very heart of nature itself, its significance is linked up with the very meaning of the world itself.

The universe is purposive. This purposiveness of reality

is concentrated in particular natures, and especially in the nature of man whose position in the scheme of things is obviously privileged in so far as he is a knowing subject. Now nature assigns to everything a curve for its life, as it were, and an object with which life enriches itself in its progress. Tendency, instinct, and in man the will-to-live, are the means whereby nature works out its purposiveness and meaning. Thus we begin to see that man's instinct for life is linked up with the entire scheme of things. Either man's will-to-live then is working toward an end or purpose or else the scheme of things entire is devoid of purpose and meaning.

But in man this will-to-live has quite a specific significance all its own. It is so ambitious in its sweep that not even time is large enough to exhaust its onward urge. Does man's will-to-live merely stretch from the cradle to the grave, or does it go out imperiously beyond the grave? This raises the further aspect of human life, its duration, which must throw a new light on life as mere existence and in its naked character.

The finest pages of literature, both ancient and modern, give echo to this indomitable hunger for life that is in the soul of man. Else, how explain the constancy with which men, ancient and modern, young and old complain of the brevity of human life? The life of man is like the inconstant shadows, like a flower that bloometh for a moment, like an arrow passing through the air, like a hurrying stream. . . . But is not brevity a relative idea? The life of man is short when compared with the life of the sun; it is long in comparison with the life of insects. Yet, all complain of it. In reality it is not the brevity of life that inspires those high plaints of man's finest literatures. If men complain because they die, it is because they would live forever. And if, in view of this desire to go on living, men are satisfied to stay and not hurry into the land of death, is it not because the instinct of immortality is strong within them and that there is in human hearts the

> . . . dread of something after death, —
> That undiscovered country, from whose bourne
> No traveller returns, — puzzles the will;
> And makes us rather bear those ills we have,
> Than fly to others that we know not of?
> Thus conscience doth make cowards of us all;
> And thus the native hue of resolution
> Is sicklied o'er with the pale cast of thought;
> And enterprises of great pitch and moment
> With this regard, their currents turn awry,
> And lose the name of action.

Shakespeare wisely philosophized on life in that immortal soliloquy of Hamlet:

> To be, or not to be; — that is the question:
> Whether 'tis nobler in the mind to suffer
> The slings and arrows of outrageous fortune,
> Or to take arms against a sea of troubles,
> And, by opposing, end them? To die: to sleep; —
> No more: and by a sleep, to say we end
> The heart-ache, and the thousand natural shocks
> That flesh is heir to; — 'tis a consummation
> Devoutly to be wished! . . . To die: to sleep: —
> To sleep? perchance to dream! — Ay, there's the rub!
> For in that sleep of death what dreams may come,
> When we have shuffled off this mortal coil,
> Must give us pause! . . .

Man's instinct for continued life, his will-to-live, "must give us pause" and make us see that a life cannot be aimless which has eternity for its goal, that the value of life is such that time is not long enough to exhaust its meaning, and that the purposes of nature and the meaning of life go hand in hand. In man the will-to-live, reaching the dimensions of an immortal aspiration, has its roots deep in life and nature, and for such a desire of nature there is the guarantee of nature's purposiveness as a whole. Either we admit the possibility of the universal frustration of nature's purposes, or we accept a final environment for human life which guarantees its purposiveness and meaning.

Human life, however, is not a mere existence or duration; nor is it of mere existence that man is enamored. If there is one truth more than another stressed by the psychology of the present day it is the conative, striving character of life; life is dynamic, not static. Human life cannot be reduced merely to responses on the part of man to external stimuli, it possesses an impulse of its own, a series of impulses in fact, and it responds to reality around it. Life is an unfolding of desire, a promise of fuller life, and by contact with the universe man hopes to enrich his life.

But will the universe around him satisfy his deep desires? Is there a single man who thinks so? A universe that can thwart his deepest instincts, which resists and fights him, which inflicts pain and misery, can such a world be the final home of one whose life is a deep desire of fuller, richer, greater life? The pessimist seeks his own way out and in his going simply asserts the greatness of his desires and the present world's incapacity to fulfill them. For pessimism is despair, and despair is hope frustrated. It is his desire for fullness of life that explains the pessimism of the pessimist.

Here then is the beginning of an answer to the question, "Is Life Worth Living?" If death is the end of all, life assuredly is not worth living. It has been frequently objected against the doctrine of a future life that, looked upon as a compensation for the present world, it canalized men's energies and directed them toward a preoccupation with the life to come instead of guiding them toward the ameliorization of the present. But the contrary objection against disbelief in a future life is even stronger. It is true that when people do not accept a future life they are pressed into making the most of the present one. But making the most of life is variously interpreted and not infrequently is it prompted by a desperate effort to exhaust, by every manner and kind of experience, legitimate or otherwise, what life seems to offer. But to ask from life what God has not put into it for man as a spiritual being tends only to disillusionment and despair. If life has meaning, then life has laws. And the man who has disregarded the laws of life may look and cry for complete cessation . . . but the mountains will not fall upon him and the cry of his deeper nature for continued life will be his torment. If, on the other hand, a man seeks from life what God intended life to offer, when moral obligation is the law of his life and virtue his highest good, even then the worth and value of life demands a future existence. Otherwise, man is the dupe of virtue. This sounds a hard saying. But as long as virtue is unrequited in this world, as long as the good suffer and the wicked prosper, we must look forward to a future life. Some may object and say that the joy of a good conscience is sufficient recompense for virtue. This objection ignores the complexity of man and the relatively small empire that belongs to conscience in the psychic life of the individual. A good conscience is a great possession, but until a good conscience has power to transmute the ills of fortune, to fill the mind with light, to erase the memory of injustices patiently borne, virtue and complete happiness do not meet. The most we can infer is that if life is to have purpose and meaning there must be a final home where integral happiness will be virtue's reward.

The question of life's meaning and purpose then will depend upon what object, or objects, a man selects for the enrichment of his life. In determining what such objects must be, the question of individual temperament is of comparatively little interest. All men are so alike in nature that a proper reading of what goes to constitute the life of man may well afford to dispense with individual differences or personal reactions. The important thing to fix upon is the essential things in the life of man. And these essentials in human life are three in number: man has a mind that hungers for truth, a will that is in search of goodness, and his life of action is under the attractiveness of beauty. Men have always recognized that the true, the good, the beautiful are the fundamental values for life. But where does truth dwell, or goodness, or beauty, if not in the Supreme Being, God?

If human life then is faced toward the heights of truth and goodness and beauty that meet in God, it can achieve its real meaning only by an acquisition of God. In Himself God is Truth and Goodness and Beauty, but for man He can be such only in so far as he can place God somehow within his life. Human life is unpossessed of real meaning that is unpossessed of God.

That is only another way of saying that life without religion is devoid of meaning. Religion stands for the linking up of human life with the pursuit of God: in that quest lies the only hope of meaning and value that the life of man possesses.

# 9

# Ancient and Modern Views of Life

It is the pretension of these pages that the significant philosophies of life that have made their appearance in the course of history are best and most conveniently divided into three distinct and characteristic outlooks. These three attitudes have been already characterized as ancient, modern, and contemporary. The ancient philosophy of life may be looked upon as elastic enough to embrace all human thought, whether philosophic or religious, from known origins to the period of its classical exponent, St. Thomas of Aquin, in the thirteenth century. The modern outlook on life dates from the sixteenth century and finds its representative spokesman in Lord Francis Bacon. This outlook runs on into our own epoch, of course, but we have already seen that the nineteenth century gave birth to a new and characteristic inquiry which exists side by side with what may be styled a typically modern philosophy of life. One may be well aware of the sweeping character of this synoptic account of the history of human thought, but these three distinct attitudes, we believe, are sufficiently definite and clear-cut to serve as a map of the route traversed by the human mind in its inquiry into the problem of human life.

So many things have been said of the modern epoch that one may legitimately fear to add to them. It is not easy to lay hold of the pure essence of a period and distill it in words. The difficulty is intensified when one bears in mind the continuity of history. History is a stream that is ever flowing: no one, said an old Greek philosopher, ever enters the same stream twice. One epoch runs riotously into another to swell the tide, and in the enlarged stream it is difficult to trace the meeting of the waters. The modern era carries forward in its bosom the contribution of every epoch that went before: the past is the matrix of the modern, as the modern is of the contemporary.

Historians, however, are not balked by this. In the course of time there are rather well-defined epochs, distinct expressions in manifold ways of a certain unity of mind and spirit. The ways of thinking and the modes of life in one particular age are not those of another. In the long run we may come to discern peak points, the road runs up into one eminence and then dips again; we miss its meanderings in the valleys until it rises up again to some new point distinct and different from the former. The result seems to be that a chasm seems to lie between one epoch and another. This much at least can be said of the ancient view of life, culminating with Aquinas, as compared with the modern view that begins with Lord Bacon and still holds the mind of many. Let it be granted then that a chasm lies between the ancient philosophy of life and the modern. Between the thirteenth and the sixteenth centuries the modern approach to life takes place.

Without entertaining any thought of sudden rupture, but of gradual disintegration and new formation, we shall not be far wrong if we say that the ancient view of life, systematized by Aquinas, looks upon Contemplation, presently to be explained, as the goal of life, whereas the modern view, expressed by Bacon and systematized by more recent thinkers, looks upon Action as the end of life. These two ideals, outlined not only by the two men we have selected but accepted by many and acted upon by the contemporaries of each, are now looked upon generally as two radically distinct and opposed conceptions of the life of man. Without endorsing the opposition, which really is not as fundamental as we are led to believe, we may take them as expressing two distinct spirits, the spirit of the ancient world as opposed to that of the modern.

On their external side the ancient (combining under this term the medieval) period and the modern present striking differences. The medieval epoch, for instance, saw Europe one externally in a sense it never has been since: the Europe of our time is a wind-swept dust of many nations. Further, on their inner side these two epochs vastly differ. Medieval Europe had a unity of culture that is lacking in modern times. The medieval epoch was a manifold expression of a single spirit that expressed itself in art, in letters, in philosophy: modern Europe has no similar unity to offer. A religious outlook on life was the unifying factor in the Middle Ages; today the consistency of that common outlook has been lost.

Of this religious outlook Aquinas may be taken as the classical exponent. He has the advantage, too, that he sums up the wisdom of all ages, now drawing on Aristotle, now on St. Augustine and through him on Plato.

Now, Aquinas proves in many places that the goal of life is contemplation. He knows by faith that man is destined for a supernatural vision of God, he knows by reason that God is the Supreme Good, and he declares that the final end of life is the vision of Truth itself. He sees the meaning of man's present life in the light of this ultimate destiny, and with convincing logic St. Thomas goes on to show that every human action, all human offices in society and in the State, humanity at large in all its avocations, express a human life that has but one goal and destiny, the vision of God.

The light of this destiny reveals the plan of man's present life. It can be acquired only by merit, by supernatural living, by a unification of all man's powers in a free choice for God and in a love without measure. St. Thomas was intellectualist enough to say that man's destiny would be vision, as opposed to other Christian thinkers, but in this life, he declared, it is better to love God than to know Him. Nor did he renounce for this life the ideal of contemplation which would be full and perfect only in the next. On the contrary, he held that already here below the goal of life was contemplation of God.

St. Thomas discusses explicitly the question of the contemplative and active life. In his time there was not the same stress on Action which came later in the sixteenth century, but the principles given by St. Thomas are sure and solid. The only priority he admits for active life is one of time. He looks upon it chiefly as a preparation for the life of contemplation which is the real goal. Thus he says that the active life is useful for the acquisition of virtue, for dominating human passion, and for acquiring a mastery over the chaotic impulses and instincts of human life. But once a certain poise and balance have been achieved, and with this calm a true human freedom to follow what is best and noblest, inevitably a desire, springing from supernatural charity, impels the Christian toward contemplation. In so far as this desire is followed, a man is brought forward toward his real destiny, the vision of God. The object of this contemplation being God Himself, and other things viewed in the light of God, it follows that here we have the supreme end of life, an end that has value in itself without reference to any extrinsic object, desirable by man in and for itself. Aquinas says explicitly that this contemplation of Truth, this supernatural union with God, this loving consideration of the divine, is an end-in-chief, intrinsically desirable and subordinate to nothing else. In this commerce with God by contemplation we have initiation in the life of heaven: human destiny has begun for man to be realized on earth. Contemplation is the goal of life that does not look beyond itself.

What then of the active life? St. Thomas, who holds that the most perfect life is a combination of contemplation and action, never stirs from his original position. Contemplation never ceases to be an end in itself; nowhere does he subordinate contemplation to action. Contemplation is never a means, not even a means for fecundating a life of action (which infallibly it does), it always ranks supreme. In what is called the "mixed" life action, envisaged by Aquinas as teaching, or preaching, or ministry (it is in relation to religious that he raises the question), action ranks as a subordinate end: contemplation is the primary business of life, action secondary.

In all this Aquinas was perfectly consistent. For him

God was the Goal of life and life was meaningless unless possessed by God. But granting that life ascends to God in charity and that the love of fellow men is an integral part of divine charity, yet God does not cease to enjoy primacy over every other interest. Accordingly, contemplation which has to do with God directly is supreme, just as love of God is primary and that of the neighbor the consequence of this love. Action, then, for St. Thomas is viewed as an extension of contemplation, not an end to which contemplation is subordinate, just as the love of one's fellow men is a prolongation of the love of God, not the end and aim of it.

The contemplative ideal demands a certain leisure and repose; it rises up enticingly before the minds of those in whose soul the flame of charity burns brightly. It begins and ends in love and its ultimate aim is a love without measure that rivets it in contemplating the beauty of God. Absolutely speaking, he says, it surpasses in excellency a life of action, and he proceeds to press Aristotle's many philosophic reasons in favor of the contemplative ideal of life into the service of Christianity. The contemplative ideal is more in keeping with the nature of God and man; it emphasizes the worth and value of God in Himself; it is more durable, more delectable, than the life of action; and as man is man by the possession of intelligence, contemplation, wherein man is carried on the wings of love to a vision of Truth in this life, is already the beginning of man's ultimate destiny.

In this vision of human life Aquinas finds a place for all creation, for every craft and trade, for every function and office of society: the order of the universe is one wherein matter, body, mind converge toward the final goal, the vision of Truth. The end of the universe is that which is intended by its Creator; but the First Cause and ultimate Source of things is the divine Intelligence. As the good of intellect, its proper object and perfection, is truth, it follows that Truth is the Supreme Object of the universe entire, and contemplation of Truth the goal of human existence at large. The thing for which men were made and live is contemplation; all things else run up into that ideal as to their final consummation. Such was the ideal systematized by Aquinas: it marks an epoch in the history of philosophies of life.

The Thomistic system as a whole was, it may be supposed, the greatest all-round synthesis that has appeared in the course of history. But with the death of Aquinas, his philosophy, so organic and unified, shared in the general disintegration of medieval culture as a whole. During the three centuries that followed his death, Europe underwent many changes; new conditions of life appeared; sciences grew up and sought autonomy; a general dissatisfaction with the philosophy of the past made itself felt; and in time the outlook on life has so changed that the contemplative ideal of life loses favor, and a new spirit appears. With the practical advance of scientific discovery men cried out against the sterility of the old philosophy: it was good for nothing. Chiefly they complained of its practical inutility, its scientific sterility, it seemed to lag behind while scientists were throwing open new doors to the mysteries of the world around them. But soon the ideal of life itself, associated with the findings of the older philosophers, became equally distasteful. Whereas the old philosophy had effected nothing apparently for the ordinary life of mortal men, it had not promoted material well-being or alleviated men's sufferings, the new scientific discoveries proved of almost immediate benefit, increasing man's power over the elements and benefiting generally the material conditions of human existence. The contemplative ideal of the Middle Ages, it was argued, tended to take men away from practical life, it directed men's interests to eternity and not to time, it seemed to leave the external conditions of life stagnant.

That an element of truth existed in many of these protests can scarcely be denied. Whether the reason of human ills was the philosophic outlook on life that made contemplation the end-in-chief, is another question. But when the reaction against medievalism commenced, it was bound ultimately to work itself out in an entirely new view of human life. Lord Francis Bacon in the sixteenth century made himself the spokesman of the new ideal that had been gradually forming in the minds of men. He caught the spirit of his age, and though his influence in scientific domains has been hugely overestimated, it is true to say that he has exercised a real and definite influence on the course of philosophic thought. He voiced the claims of discovery as the end of science, he taxed the old philosophy with a complete misreading of the end of knowledge, he urged the importance of invention, but above all he emphasized utility as the real goal of all scientific endeavor. His originality lies in the fact that he is the spokesman of an epoch. Bacon certainly caught the temper of his age, and served to give human thought a drift away from what he considered sterile contemplation to action, action on nature, discovery of ideas and instruments, and the bending of all human knowledge to man's use and benefit. He was too near the Middle Ages not to pay some homage to contemplation, but his homage was only halfhearted. For Bacon knowledge was no end in itself, it was power or nothing, and contemplation was subordinate to action. He had no time for disinterested contemplation: contemplation became a species of discovery, the finding of new ideas which in their turn would be instruments of action.

Bacon found his Boswell in Macaulay, who in a graphic account of Bacon's contribution to philosophy extolled his role and influence. Never before the time of Bacon, says Macaulay, was the true end and aim of knowledge rightly grasped. "The chief peculiarity of Bacon's philosophy," wrote Macaulay, "seems to have been this, that it aimed at things altogether different from those which his predecessors had proposed to themselves." In this Macaulay was re-echoing Bacon, who claimed the same honor for himself. The more carefully indeed the works of Bacon are examined, the more clearly it appears that the results intended by him were radically different from the medieval outlook. The end that Bacon put before him was, to employ his own emphatic word, "fruit." It was the multiplying of human enjoyments, the mitigating of human suffering, "the relief of man's estate." This, says Macaulay, was the object of all his speculations in every department of science, in natural philosophy, in legislation, in politics, in morals.[1] The older philosophers "promised what was impracticable; they despised what was practicable; they filled the world with long words and long beards; and they left it as wicked and as ig-

---

[1] See Essay on Lord Bacon, *Essays*, 1914, p. 392.

norant as they found it."[2] "Two words form the key of the Baconian doctrine, utility and progress."[3]

Already the direction that this outlook on life, as expressed by Bacon, is taking is clearly discernible. Nobody could quarrel with the emphasis on progress and on scientific discovery: already in the Middle Ages the beginnings of scientific interest are clearly noticeable in Roger Bacon and Albert the Great. But it is the opposition between contemplation and action that is becoming a menace to clear thinking. Before Bacon, said Macaulay, man was made for philosophy; since Bacon, philosophy is for man. But the real nature of man is being forgotten. With this reaction man is definitely turned away from the goal of contemplation, which was looked upon as sterile, to the new ideal of the conquest of nature, increased power, and action. The end of life is definitely not contemplation in any sense: the goal of life is action.

The logical issue of this trend of thought is a system of philosophy known as Pragmatism. Pragmatism, of course, is a philosophy of life, a philosophy that takes to their logical conclusion the views of Bacon. A modern Pragmatist, John Dewey, pays tribute to Bacon as the great forerunner of the spirit of modern life, a man who has scarcely received due recognition, he remarks, as the real founder of modern thought.[4] Pragmatism is here implicitly equated with the spirit of modern thought. The word was first employed in 1878 by C. S. Peirce and for him the all-important thing in life is action. The activity of thought, he says, tends to rest in a belief because it is

[2]*Ibid.*, p. 402.
[3]*Ibid.*, p. 392.
[4]*Reconstruction in Philosophy*, p. 28.

only then we have a sure guide to our actions in object. Beliefs are simply rules of action, and thought's exclusive function is the production of active habits. All ideas that fail to determine any difference in the practical result of thought form no true and proper part of its meaning. That is but a step on the way to saying that the whole value of any idea lies in the consequences for practical life of that idea. With William James this step is taken, and he identifies the true with the useful and the opportune. "The whole function of philosophy," says William James, "ought to be to find out what definite difference it will make to you and me, at definite instants of our lives, if this world-formula or that world-formula be the true one."[5]

Papini also caught the spirit of this new outlook and in one of his tempestuous pages he tells us how "for long years (many years, many months, days and nights!) I was faithful to thee [philosophy], like the knight in the *chanson de geste,* and I had no other God before me. . . . To thee, Philosophy, I owe all. . . . And I repudiated thee — was unfaithful to thee. Thou wast but an obstacle in the way of my 'action.' Thou didst not fulfill thy promises and thy fulfillment had ceased to be of any consequence to me. I sought action, to do and change (the reality of to-day advances towards the reality of to-morrow) and thou gavest me unfruitful contemplation, the quiet of the Absolute or the exhausting fever of impatient dashings against an empty goal."[6] Later he announces the program of his new philosophy, "the philosophy of action, of doing and also of re-doing, transforming, creat-

---

[5] *Pragmatism,* p. 50.
[6] *A Man Finished,* pp. 193, 194.

ing. No more waste of time over problems that are insoluble, or paths that lead nowhere, amidst the traps and mazes of visionary dialecticians. *True* equals *useful*. *To know* equals *to do*."[7]

This is a good expression of the modern outlook on life as opposed to the ancient. Human life is definitely faced toward action, its back is turned upon first principles, upon contemplation, upon God as the Primal Source. The idea of God as Source, says W. James, has no meaning, whatever value may be accorded Him as Remunerator. "The attitude of pragmatism," this writer says, "is the attitude of looking away from first things, principles, categories, supposed necessities, and of looking towards last things, fruits, consequences, facts."[8]

Only in an age taught by Bacon, as exponent of the modern spirit, could a system like Pragmatism find favor. Pragmatism is a logical issue, but it is also a condemnation of the primacy of action over contemplation. Pragmatism will have it that reality is amorphous, that it is transformable by means of action. The world is not an objective order of things, it is in process of gradual working up, in accordance with human needs. Purpose makes the object; interest or need constitutes reality. The plain man will not easily accept this view of reality as a plastic stuff that can be ordered and arranged at will. When William James tells us that "often enough our faith beforehand in an uncertified result is the only thing that makes the result come true," our own experience tells us that such a belief is not always an invariable prelude to success. Ultimately W. James truly, though inconsistently,

[7] *Ibid.*
[8] *Pragmatism*, p. 55.

admits the "facts are the bounds of human knowledge set for it, not by it."[9] Something does exist independently of our subjective activities and which not infrequently is a resistance to our wills.

Likewise, when another pragmatist, Dr. Schiller, says that "there are truths, but no Truth," we are left unconvinced. Truth is. Truth imposes itself. We know that God is Truth, that He exists, that He is Transcendent. Grant that, and the end of life must be contemplation of Truth either directly or indirectly. The only way of harmonizing thought and action is to look at man and read his destiny aright. It is true to say that both philosophy and action are for man, and man himself is a being that seeks his full and final perfection. But precisely to subordinate contemplation to action, to make action supreme, is to miss the unique goal of human life, which is the vision of Truth Subsistent.

---

[9] *The Will to Believe*, p. 59.

# 10

# The Contribution of Christ

Christianity brought into the world an original revelation of God to Man. It threw a new light on the Mystery of Mysteries that human minds had of themselves never glimpsed. Plato and Aristotle sensed the upward movement of human minds and spirits to the Primal Source of things. Aristotle saw in God the Desired of all creation who moved the sun and stars by His attraction. Plato conceived Him vaguely as the Object that inspired the return of humanity in love to the celestial regions. But the God of Aristotle, more clearly delineated than the God of Plato, was Himself unmoved in any sense; to insure His immutability Aristotle denied Him any knowledge of contingent happenings in the material universe. Entirely absent from both is the idea of God revealed by Christ, the view of God's descent from celestial regions into this earth of ours, the love of God for man, the divine *Agape* of which the Apostles speak.

To this extent the "glad tidings" of Christianity was nothing less than revolutionary; it burst upon a world of darkness like some new sun or planet. Such a revelation of God could not have appeared without at the same time affecting human nature and human values in themselves. How could human nature be quite the same again once God united Himself to it in the Person of Jesus Christ? This conjunction of the divine and human in Christ was no passing thing either. It lasted not merely thirty-three years, the period of His earthly career, but for all eternity God in Christ will be divine and human. He ascended into heaven, man and God, and there takes His rightful place for endless ages. The Desired of all time is now a God-Man, Christ.

In itself the Incarnation is the most astounding testimony of the value of human nature. Of all possible natures God selected that of man for Hypostatic Union. Had His predilection stopped at that, man should need no other proof of worth and dignity. But the downward descent of the divine *Agape* was not exhausted in the Incarnation: Redemption was the end and object of Christ's appearance. Christ will be the Intermediary between the distant Divinity and man's nothingness aggravated by his sinfulness. From the Crucified there falls on the uplifted face of man, conscious of his nothingness, tempted by disquietude, harried by his sufferings, a stream of inundating goodness. The torrent of divine love, the goodness of the distant God, condescends to take notice of man: the Christ is Mediator between nothingness and the All. "Condescends" is scarcely the word to express the downward rush of this torrent that took the way of suffering and of blood. "It is by means of the blood which drops on this nothingness that the vitalizing emanation from God instills itself therein, and forthwith from below rises the beatitude of eternity which breaks forth shining on the face of nothingness and reascends in streams of joy toward the distant Divinity. The path by which the joy mounts is that by which the blood descended."[1]

What has Christ done? He has poured into a new humanity His own life of Godhead. What He was by nature, Son of God, He has shared with humanity by the life of grace. Like His own conjunction with human nature, this participated divinity that is of humanity redeemed is not for any period of time. Because Christ Himself has risen from the dead, so will Christians rise at some future date, not only in the spiritual part of them, their souls, but in their integrity, soul and body. "I am the resurrection and the life; he that believeth in Me, although he be dead, shall live. And everyone that liveth, and believeth in Me, shall not die forever."[2] More men and women have been convinced by this simple affirmation of Christ as to survival and immortality than by the most powerful proofs of immortality given by mortal minds. For men and women want their present life in all its integrity, soulful and corporeal, and in Christianity alone is there the solace that this instinctive feeling needs.

It is not too much to say, then, that in revealing God to man, Christ for the first time revealed man to himself in his true light. The German philosopher, Hegel, went so far as to say that with Christianity man first discovered himself as a personality. "Entire quarters of the world, Africa and the East, have never had, and have not yet, this idea. The Greeks and Romans, Plato and Aristotle and the Stoics had it not. It came into the world with

---

[1]Hoornaert, R., *The Burning Soul of St. John of the Cross*, p. 6.
[2]John 11:25, 26.

Christianity, in which the individual, as such, had an infinite worth, as being the aim and object of divine charity." This perhaps is an exaggerated statement, though in the recognition of woman's personality Christianity does mark a definite stage of progress. But what is entirely certain is that Christianity initiates a new era in the real significance of human personality. "Christian philosophy," writes M. J. Maritain, "tells us that the person is a complete individual substance, intellectual in nature and master of its actions, *sui juris, autonomous,* in the authentic sense of the word. And so the word *person* is reserved for substances which possess that divine thing, the spirit, and are in consequence, each by itself, a world above the whole bodily order, a spiritual and moral world which, strictly speaking is not a *part* of this universe, and whose secret is hidden even from the natural perception of the angels. The word *person* is reserved for substances which, choosing their end, are capable of themselves deciding on the means, and of introducing series of new events into the universe by liberty; for substances which can say after their kind, *fiat,* and it is so. And what makes their dignity, what makes their personality, is just exactly the subsistence of the spiritual and immortal soul and its supreme independence in regard to all fleeting imagery and all the machinery of sensible phenomena. Hence St. Thomas teaches that the word *person* signifies the noblest and highest thing in all nature: *persona significat id quod est perfectissimum in tota natura.*"[3] With such a view of personality it was impossible to look upon the cosmic process as a mere mechanical one or human consciousness as the mere outcome of blind forces. The human person was in

---

[3]Maritain, *Three Reformers,* pp. 19–21.

no conceivable way a product, except of God, and was therefore essentially subordinate to no human society or organization, but was subject to God alone.

But it is the dimensions of man's destiny, as revealed by Christ, that constitute Christ's real contribution to the problem of life's worth and value. Not only did He reveal man to himself as a person, with personal immortality, but Christ revealed a goal for life the like of which no human mind could have ever clearly grasped. His teaching may be summed up by saying that He came into the world with a twofold message for human life, to offer men a vision of God in eternity, and to call men to the pursuit of that vision in time.[4] More, His own lifework was consecrated to making this supernatural goal a real possibility for man. This was to throw new light on cosmic processes and human history. "But if mind," says Mr. C. Dawson, "is the key to reality and the cosmic process has a spiritual significance, then we should expect that the most permanent things in the world would be not atoms or elements, but persons, and there would be nothing shocking to the reason in the belief that the goal of the cosmic process was to be found in an order which restored and preserved that which was spiritually valuable in the present world. The human animal is no more capable of comprehending the purpose of the world by the light of his practical experience than the ant that crawls on the pylon of a wireless station is capable of understanding the meaning of radio telegraphy. And the world to come — *saeculum venturum* — may be no less different from the world of our sensible experience than is a sym-

---

[4]See Kirk, K. E., *The Vision of God* (Bampton Lectures).

phony of Beethoven from the complicated mechanism which has been framed to transmit it."[5]

This central doctrine of Christianity has become so much a part of our Christian patrimony that we scarcely realize the absolute newness of it when it was first preached by Christ Himself. Let us touch on the far-reaching implications of the Christian contribution in order: its teaching on the goal of life, the personal immortality implied, and the enlargement of the present life that follows necessarily.

That the goal of life was some kind of vision in eternity may have been the vague dream of a few philosophers derived possibly from religious sources. Plato does give the impression that he entertained the idea of a future vision of the Ocean of uncreated Beauty, but, even so, Plato has in mind merely the contemplation of the world of Ideas, and the vagueness of his teaching is intensified by the mythical form in which it is conveyed. Life, as Plato saw it, was a cycle of reincarnations, and happiness in this life was memory of vision and in the future the return to some form of pristine contemplation. Aristotle is much less daring than Plato. For him supreme happiness belongs to God alone; on earth anything corresponding to it was the privilege of the few aristocrats of thought, the philosophers, whom Aristotle, typical Greek that he was, had in view.

Strange as it may seem, there is comparatively little progress in the revelation of God as it is found in the Old Testament. From the time of Jacob down, there is a certain traditional idea of the vision of God, but to this

---

[5] *After Death* (Spectator Booklets, III), pp. 45–46.

day interpreters will dispute as to what precisely this vision implied.[6] The vision of God imparted to Jacob, Moses, Isaias, Ezechiel,[7] is surrounded with such a wealth of imagery in the Biblical account that its precise meaning is not easily grasped. We have explicit statements to the effect that no man could see God and live, and the tribe of Levi, we are told, disappeared for having seen Him.[8] It is by no means certain then that vision of God as spoken of in the Old Testament really means vision. More often it dwindles down to a vivid consciousness of Him in His chosen place of worship. When the psalmist sings of seeing God he is thinking not infrequently of the privilege of being in the Temple to enjoy God's special presence.

When it is question of a future life, where this vision might be expected really to be consummated, the Old Testament is surprisingly unenlightening. We cannot forget that the memory of Judaism was filled with the expulsion from Paradise of Adam and Eve. Created immortal, man ruined his hopes by sin. After death, what? Job's answer is sad enough: "Shall not the fewness of my days be ended shortly? Suffer me, therefore, that I may lament my sorrow a little while: Before I go, and return no more, to a land that is dark and covered with the mist of death, and no order, but everlasting horror dwelleth."[9] Death inspired them as a quasi-annihilation. "For there is no one in death," says the psalmist, "that is mindful of Thee: and who shall confess Thee in hell?"[10] "What

---

[6]Gen. 32:30; Exod. 33:11.
[7]Ezech. 10:18; 11:22; 43:2.
[8]Num. 12:6-8.
[9]Job 10:20-22.
[10]Ps. 6:6.

profit is there in Thy blood whilst I go down to corruption? Shall dust confess to Thee, or declare Thy truth?"[11] Accordingly, we have an emphasis on the present life, an appeal for longevity, on the plea that little good accrues to God from those who die. For the dead are "Like the slain sleeping in sepulchers, whom Thou rememberest no more: and they are cast off from Thy hand,"[12] whereas the living can at least praise the Almighty: "The dead shall not praise Thee, O Lord: nor any of them that go down to hell. But we that live bless the Lord: from this time now and forever."[13] All that is certain from the Old Testament is that there is a future life, that man does not cease with the death of his body, but the nature and conditions of this future life are dim and obscure.[14]

It is against the background of this dark picture, left us by the Old Testament, and the nebulous eternity of pagan philosophers that we can appraise the contribution of Jesus Christ to the problem of human destiny. His teaching is radically new, the divine largesse is thrown into relief, and the ultimate horizon of human life is seen to be a face-to-face vision of the Godhead in eternity. Christ promises that by observing certain conditions men will ultimately come to "see" God, their recompense will be great in heaven,[15] men shall be like to angels who behold God's glory.[16]

Here was a goal of life that could never have been clearly thought by the human mind. As the actual destiny

---

[11]Ps. 29:10.
[12]Ps. 87:5.
[13]Ps. 113:18.
[14]Cf. 1 Sam. 28:8–19; Gen. 25:6–10; Job 14:13–17; 19:23.
[15]Matt. 5:12.
[16]Matt. 17:10.

of men, it could never have entered into their calculations. For it is a culmination of life that is strictly beyond human nature's powers; it transcends the powers of all created and finite intelligences. As such it depended absolutely on God's own choice to bestow, and Christ who was God revealed to men that this real and actual destiny in eternity was nothing short of seeing God face to face. He made it possible by dying and by infusing into human spirits a principle of life that made man connatural, as it were, with God, thereby putting him on the way of finally coming to God in the intimacy of vision.

Having thus clarified the goal of human existence and implicitly assured men of immortality, Christ cast a new light on the present life of men on earth. For this eternal life, He pointed out, was already to begin in time. But the striking thing in this contribution of Christ is the embraciveness of His message. He came to call *all* men to vision, and therefore to offer to humanity at large a supernatural destiny. The significance of this largesse on the part of God must not be missed. The Jewish people had looked upon themselves as a chosen people; the Greek philosophers had in mind only certain aristocrats of thought for whom any decent destiny was intended. The Jew put a premium, as indeed God Himself had done, on race; the Greek upon intelligence. But Christ was universal in His appeal: He preached His doctrine to the gentiles, and ignored, or seemed temporarily to ignore, the aristocracy of mind and talent.

To every man, whether Jew or Gentile, whether learned or ignorant, was offered a goal of life that surpassed all knowing and yet was vision. "We shall be like Him *because* we shall see Him as He is."[17] Like to God, then, but not absorbed by God, just as human nature did not cease to be itself in its espousals with the Word. Further, human personality, of no matter what nation or level of intelligence, can be enhanced by becoming one with Christ and "sharing the divine nature"[18] with Him. By Baptism into Christ the Christian is sealed with Christ, is marked with Him, yet remains himself. The Christian is a man convinced that he will never fully find himself, achieve his highest and fullest perfection, until he sees himself "in Christ." In Christ lies for him the hope of Resurrection not only in the spiritual part of him, but in his body also. "For the keynote of the Christian doctrine of the future life is not Immortality, but Resurrection; not the survival of an immaterial principle, but the vital restitution of human nature in its integrity."[19]

---

[17] I John 3:2.
[18] 2 Pet. 1:4.
[19] Dawson, C., *loc. cit.*

## 11

# The Plasticity of Life

Having vindicated the purposiveness of human life, we must now return to examine what may be called the fundamental presupposition of life's value for every man. It may be well to give a map of life, indicating the far-off hills for which the course of life is set, but it is still more important to convince a man that of many possible routes he may select the one that will take him finally to his goal. Some people seem to think that man mechanically marches along the roads of life, or that he is pushed or drawn blindfold along his path. "We may or may not be free," says one writer, "but we move all the same."

Life in all its levels reveals itself as some form of spontaneous energy, capable of adaptation to changing circumstances, and so far the effort to interpret it after the analogy of a machine has not succeeded. Still more true does this appear of life as it belongs to man. The average man is conscious that within certain limits his life is plastic and that he can fashion it after the visionings of his mind. It is quite unnecessary to exaggerate this plasticity to the extent of ridding life of all determining influences. In early life the little child instinctively reacts to its environment; all through life men are aware of the urge of instinctive life within them. But to the question whether life is lived for him by unknown and uncontrollable forces, or whether as a human person he can live his life to a certain extent, the average man has no uncertain answer: he knows that he can introduce unity and pattern into his life and that where ultimate issues are in question he is master of his destiny. At some period it comes home to him that he can be an artist in a stupendous sense, an artist of his own life. His visionings of life he can impress upon all that is plastic in him and finally succeed in making of it a thing of beauty.

Without this initiative of the human person, this power of man to choose the pattern of his own life, the value and purposiveness of human life can have little import. If life is lived *for* man rather than *by* him, if he is just a thing among other objects of creation, if he is swept along in some great current of life, he may well dispense himself from the effort of mapping out life's hills and hollows: the question of life's ultimate goal has no real concern for him. If man is not free, then he is simply a moment in the general life of things, he is no more the maker of his destiny than is the animal, and life is not plastic in his hands, no matter how variable it may seem to be.

The alternative here, then, narrows down to the old question of free will and what is called determinism. To accept freedom is to believe in man's initiative, in life's plasticity, and to hold that a man is capable of substituting actions of his own free choice for those activities that would appear in his life if man were not free. Man has always been looked upon as a "maker"; he can fashion instruments, modify the world around him, work up its plastic matter into monuments of art. But St. Thomas and the Scholastics have distinguished two kinds of "making" corresponding to the words *facere* and *agere*. For them action is applicable not only to man's preoccupations with the outside world, but also to forms of action which do not envisage external products but have their term in man himself; they recognized an inner world in man himself and looked upon it as subject to man's powers, capable of being "made" upon the pattern of his vision. They ascribed to man not only the power of vision but the capacity to order and regulate the activities of his inner life upon the pattern of his choice. The determinist is one who refuses to acknowledge this. He denies that man can rule or govern the conditions of his life or inform the energies of life with any unity suggested by his mind: life is lived for man rather than by him.

The average man does not take determinism seriously. He may recognize at times that such a doctrine would have a certain convenience for him, but no amount of wishing can easily convince him. He goes on believing, knowing, that he is free. He has, in fact, an uneasy feeling that if he is not more free in actual life, the fault is somehow his own. He recognizes that freedom can be increased and with a sigh acknowledges that he is responsible for his very lack of freedom. Freedom stands for man in his dignity of human personality and he who clings to the value of his person tacitly admits his prerogative of freedom. If man is a person, autonomous in a right sense, essentially subordinate to no finite institution, not even strictly a part of this cosmos in which he lives, then his claim for personality must be substantiated by his claim to freedom as a subsistent rational nature and not merely an object or thing among other things.

But what of the determinist? Are we to disbelieve the words of writers who hold that man is not free to fashion his life? In reality the matter is not quite as simple as that. We have every right to be suspicious of those who suavely write that we may or may not be free. To take refuge in such a possible deception of ourselves by some evil genius is simply shirking facts. When others deny human freedom we must look beyond the immediate denial to see what prompts. Very frequently the denial is inspired by the exigencies of some system already accepted. If a man is a pure materialist he *has* to be a determinist to be logical. But then we see no reason why a man must be a materialist; on the contrary, we see every reason why he should not be. If he prefers the logic of a system, let him: we prefer to look again at the facts. As for those who are mere speculative determinists, denying freedom because of some imagined speculative difficulty, we must meet them in practice. It will not be the first instance of men who are complex enough to preach in theory what they deny in practice. In practice the most rigorous determinist denies his determinism.

The logical determinist holds that everything in life is the result of blind fatality, that everything he does he *must* do, but in actual life he is constantly giving the lie to his theory. Does he mean to insist, for instance, that his holding determinism, and my admitting freedom, is something absolutely inevitable for both of us? If so, then life plays strangely with us. Does he mean that it is fate that he should be a determinist and that I should in this fashion be arguing against him, or that I should be allowed to do so through the kindness of certain publishers? It is a pity that when men theorize they should lose sight of facts. Liberty is a fact and a fact of this kind is worth a thousand systems. If man is what he appears immediately to be, a thinking subject, he is free even when he denies his freedom: who compels him, or what, to affirm or deny?

If freedom of the will is a fact, what objection can prevail against it? It is a fact of which I am as immediately conscious as of any other intimate fact of my experience. It is a fact of which one can lose consciousness only to the extent that one ceases to look upon oneself as a person. It is always a bad practice to mortgage facts on the basis of theorizing, and such an immediate fact of consciousness as freedom may be denied only on the basis of some false idea of freedom.

If it is held, for instance, that free will means the consciousness of an arbitrary power of choice, of acting without any reason or motive, then one is well on the way to denying the existence of such a power in man. We are conscious of our mental faculties only in so far as they show themselves in action, and in action we are well aware that we act for motives. Every action requires two causes, that which produces it and that for which it is performed, and volition is no exception: it demands a will, as efficient cause, but the final cause, that for which or on account of which the will acts, is the object willed. It is as impossible to have a volition without an object as it is to have a movement that goes nowhere. When a man wills, therefore, he must will something: that much at least is to be said in favor of determinism.

But it is precisely here that determinists and those in favor of free will join issue. For what object is it which moves the will, and has every object power to do so? Like intellect, the human will has its own proper object. The adequate object of the human intellect is being or reality considered as truth. But the human will shares in this outlook of intelligence, and for it the adequate object of all its actions is being or reality considered as good. Now, just as it would be absurd to introduce limits into the object of intelligence, since being is that which considered in itself is illimited, so the adequate object of the will enjoys the same latitude and extent. If truth in general is the object of intellect, so the good in general is that of will. In regard to this object the will is not free; everything it wills must be as participated goodness; it is set, so to speak, to capture goodness.

The human will, then, is determined in relation to this ultimate goodness and, being a universal tendency, it is always, as it were, in act regarding the universal good. That being so, it is quite evident that the will as a faculty of choice can never be determined by any particular object that is likely to come up for consideration. But that is only another way of saying that there is never any particular motive which will explain a man's choice fully. Why? Because against any particular object or motive there is the pull exerted by the universal good which by its nature the will desires. Were it necessary for the will to await a determining influence which would remove its indifference to particular objects, the will should never act. If then as a matter of experience man is constantly acting, selecting different objects and various lines of conduct, the reason must be that the will's indetermination in regard to particular objects has been removed. But since nothing outside of it is capable of doing this, it must be admitted that the will removes its own indetermination, that it is a faculty of auto-determination, man himself being the reason for his willing this or that. That is what is meant by freedom.

It is this freedom which alone explains man's sense of responsibility. If a man were not free, then his consciousness of being responsible in certain circumstances is inexplicable. When a person takes it upon himself to decide on a particular course of action he is conscious that he himself is the real reason for his actions. When a man declares himself responsible for any given action, he puts himself forward as the immediately supreme explanation of that particular action. Implicitly he declares his own freedom.

It is sometimes argued that a man must act for the strongest motive, but, apart from instances where it is clearly a case of equal motives for and against, it is frequently forgotten that it is the will itself which must render the motive strongest. It is just the prerogative of the will as free that it selects its object where no particular object could possibly be the final reason for its willing. Set a billiard ball moving along a table, it *must* go, except it is impeded, in a determined direction, but the human will in presence of two routes to be traversed can choose either one or the other because it is not determined to one or the other. Granting that the will, as a faculty of nature, is determined by the ultimate goal of life, yet in action it shows itself to be a faculty of choice, selecting freely the means that supposedly lead to the acquisition of the ultimate end.

These are considerations that are not far removed from the life of men. All men feel impelled by an inner urge toward a supreme Object, completion of some kind. But the routes taken by men are various: some place the goal of life in God, others in wealth, others in pleasure. As a man is, so will the supreme thing in life appear to him to be. Even theoretically the views of men on what is the supreme good of life are many. And all this goes to show the indetermination there necessarily is in life. Deeper still, the multiplicity of moral systems that have seen the light in the course of human history testify to an interest in the ideal of life which is inconsistent with determinism. In all such systems there is an effort to indicate what human life *ought* to be. But if life is absolutely determined for men, why speak of what *ought* to be?

Philosophy has been usually divided into two great branches, speculative and practical. To practical philosophy belongs the general problem of life and conduct. Life and action suggest unfinished things, development and growth; they await an order to be discovered and a unity to be realized. It is the task of practical philosophy to indicate that order that must be achieved by men in life if their lives are to be really human. Like all science, practical philosophy takes its rise in facts, and the fact with which it starts may be called the "moral fact." What is covered by the "moral fact" is simply that spontaneously men characterize human conduct as good or evil, they consider it as subject of praise and blame, and thereby affirm their belief in man's freedom and responsibility.

The distinction between "explaining" human conduct and "excusing" it has never been obliterated. There may be for a man's behavior a thousand reasons but not a single excuse, as Kipling would say; and in this distinction, as well as in the correlative praise or blame that goes with it, lies the instinctive belief of men in human freedom and responsibility.

# 12

# Optimism or Pessimism?

In constructing a philosophy of life one of the ultimate problems that one has to solve is the age-long conflict of optimism and pessimism; one has to ask whether one's interpretation of human life leads to optimism or pessimism. It is difficult to see why this should be so, and why a philosophy of life is to be judged by whether it is going to engender an optimistic or a pessimistic outlook on the world. Is the alternative of optimism or pessimism above and beyond the alternative of truth and error, or must an interpretation of experience, though true, take second place in regard to the supposedly more ultimate alternative of optimism or pessimism?

The matter is complicated by the unsatisfactory forms of optimism and pessimism with which we are acquainted in the lives of many individuals with whom our lot is cast. The problem here is largely a matter of temperament. Some are born optimists and seem to see life through rose-colored spectacles; the born pessimist sees life under a perpetual cloud of darkness; those who are

natively endowed with right good sense find themselves
in constant danger from having to live with either, for
though the pessimist scarcely helps, a certain type of optimist infallibly produces pessimism on his whole en-
tourage.

No solution is likely to accrue as long as we rest on the
level of purely individual or temperamental reactions. For
some life is rose-colored, for others drab; and there's an
end of it. We are looking for a rational outlook and we
are offered a mood. Papini recalls a period of his life when
the dark cloud of pessimism seemed to settle over it: "At
that period of my life," he says, "the eternal and utterly
useless question kept recurring to my mind in the selfsame words in which it has been clad throughout all time:
*'Is Life Worth Living?'* What could my answer be? Life
held little promise for me and was giving me nothing."[1]
There are moods in the life of every individual when a
similar reaction suggests itself . . . but the moods pass,
the sky clears, and life is worth living again.

> Is life worth living? Yes, so long
> As Spring revives the year,
> And hails us with the cuckoo's song,
> To show that she is here;
> So long as May or April takes,
> In smiles and tears, farewell,
> And windflowers dapple all the brakes,
> And primroses the dell . . .

Memory may be given to us to recapture spring in
winter, but the memory of certain individuals may have
room only for the winter of their discontent. When the

---

[1] *A Man Finished,* pp. 53–54.

French poet, Anna de Noailles, looking backward on her
life sums it up as:

> Rien. Partout l'éphemère et partout le risible,
> Partout l'insulte au coeur, partout la surdité,
> J'examine ce soir ma vie âpre et compacte:
> J'ai fait ce que j'ai pu, d'un haut et triste coeur,
> Sachant que mes peines et beaucoup des actes
> Ont sombré à jamais, sans bruit et sans lueur.

"Nothing. Everywhere the ephemeral and everywhere the laugh-
able, everywhere insult to the heart, and deafness. I examine this
evening my life, rough but compact. I have done what I could,
with a heart uplifted and sad, knowing that my sorrows and many
of my acts have perished forever, noiseless and without casting
any light."

we have at most a poetic expression of what one lady's
individual reaction to life has been; the question still remains whether life must necessarily have been so for her.

In arguing for a certain plasticity in human life we have
been vindicating the role that freedom and initiative may
play in the art of human living. But, even granting liberty,
we know that life may offer obstacles to human creativeness, that facts are stubborn, that the intermeddling of
chance and fate, as it seems to the individual, still leaves
room for questioning. But the difficulty is that the alternative of optimism or pessimism is not subject to rough-
and-ready solutions and that from certain viewpoints the
alternative simply gives rise to problems that are insoluble. It is essential then to fix on what is the meaning of
the alternative.

It is quite evident, for instance, that if the solution is to
depend on the individual's experience of life he shall have
long to wait before he can make up his mind: he would

need to be in a position to survey a long past and compute it in his own terms. But meanwhile the task of life must be faced, and one needs a certain amount of optimism for that. Further, what are his terms going to be, upon what basis is he going to decide, and what is he to regard as the factors which will weigh in forming optimism or pessimism? Then again, to pronounce on human life one would have to decide not on the life of one man's experience but for all, for life is the affair of all humanity, so that the problem begins to assume gigantic dimensions. And if life goes out beyond this sphere of things, how is its value to be computed by a mere glance at time?

More important than all other considerations is that to judge of the value of life one must have a standard of value, something which decides whether things are contributing to an optimistic or a pessimistic view. Only too frequently the problem suggests itself in terms of pleasure and it is tacitly supposed that pleasure is the supreme value. But before this can be taken for granted it must be decided whether life is for pleasure and whether pleasure is to be ranked as the one thing which gives life meaning. It may be said that optimism and pessimism are determined by men's views on what for them is the real significance of life.

The question, *Is Life Worth Living?*, is not as devoid of meaning as Papini would have us believe. For, as Chesterton suggests, sorrow which is part of life is always based upon the loss of certain things that have value, whereas pessimism is based on the conviction that nothing has value at all. This attitude of the pessimist may be due originally to a false ideal of life that is shattered by life's actual history, but on last analysis the problem depends on whether life has meaning and value despite the obvious evils that impede the path of man. But if life *has* a meaning, then radical pessimism is excluded.

This does not mean that we must rush into an exaggerated optimism. Extremes of pessimism or optimism are equally distasteful to reason. When Schopenhauer thinks that this is the worst possible world, or Leibnitz that it is the best possible world, we can dismiss both of them: the worst possible and the best possible are equally impossible when we remember the infinite number of possible worlds. There is a sense in which man himself is a key to the world in which he lives, and only by looking squarely at man himself can we decide. Optimism of any kind can be justified only by the full consciousness of the actual state of things in the world. If with this consciousness there is still room for the belief that life's highest values can be, and will be realized, the extreme of an ill-advised despair may be excluded.

The actual state of man is not such as to produce that light-hearted confidence which believes that all is well with him. Patmore once wrote

> The whole of life is womanhood to thee
> Momently wedded with enormous bless,

but he was not thinking of man. Far other is the life of man, and it is just man's torment that life can be so many things to him besides "a womanhood of enormous bless." It is just the enigma of life that its forms are Protean, passing from moods of gentleness to the fiercer moods of man and beast. Nor is it merely a thing of changing suc-

cessive moods, but a complicated thing of many forms all
at once. At any moment there may be strain and tension.
The eternal human fact is that man within him is divided
and a prey to the conflict of good and evil, of flesh and
spirit, of self and not-self. Arnold may complain:

> Affections, Instincts, Principles and Powers,
> Impulse and Reason, Freedom and Control —
> So men, unravelling God's harmonious whole,
> Rend in a thousand shreds this life of ours.

But where does man's "majestic unity," as he calls it, reside? The division of man's being, for the most part the
source of his every ill, is too elemental a fact of human
life to be denied. Empty the world's literature of this
theme, and what have you?

There are moments of visitation when man's aspiration
goes out to the noble, the pure, the good:

> How could I praise thee, Lord . . .
> If what my soul doth feel sometimes
> My soul might ever feel; . . .
>
>            might mortal breath
> Express the passion then inspired,
> Evil would die a natural death
> And nothing transient be desired.

At other times there are subterranean gusts of passion that
seem to threaten all that is good and noble. Man's life is
like that. In him flesh and spirit are finely wed, not so
finely as to exclude all discord, yet finely enough to exalt
the flesh by spirit's enthusiasms and to lower spirit by

body's needs. From mood to mood man scarcely recognizes himself; to be torn between them is the torment of his life.

To a great extent this torment is the source of human suffering, for it is just the power of passion that it induces that separation of self from self which is the cause of strife and hatred.

> To fly from, need not be to hate mankind,
> All are not fit with them to stir and toil
> Nor is it discontent to keep the mind
> Deep in its fountain, lest it overboil
> In the hot throng, where we become the spoil
> Of our infection, till too late and long
> We may deplore and struggle with the coil
> In wretched interchange from wrong to wrong
> Midst a contentious world, striving where none are strong.

There is a sense of separateness when the earth becomes a place of agony and strife, agony for a self whose ambition outruns its power of achievement, strife for a separate self which strives against the self of others. All the "complexes" that psychologists find in life translate in some way the inner discord that is at the heart of life.

There are times when the calm and balance of the world around him serves but to emphasize man's own lack of unity. The universe seems ordered, it calmly works out its appointed destiny, and animals live peacefully . . . but even the universe bears the marks of man's inner discord:

> All is seared with trade; bleared, smeared with toil;
> And wears man's smudge and shares man's smell.

"The sight of the world," wrote Newman, "is nothing

else than the prophet's scroll, full of lamentations, and mourning, and woe! To consider the world in its length and breadth, its various history, the many races of man, their starts, their fortunes, their mutual alienation, their conflicts; and then their ways, habits, governments, forms of worship; their enterprises, their aimless courses, their random achievements and acquirements, the impotent conclusion of long-standing facts, the tokens so faint and broken of a superintending design, the blind evolution of what turn out to be great truths, the progress of things, as if from unreasoning elements, not toward final causes, the greatness and littleness of man, his far-reaching aims, his short duration, the curtain hung over his futurity, the disappointments of life, the defeat of the good, the success of evil, physical pain, mental anguish, the prevalence and intensity of sin, the pervading idolatries, the corruptions, the dreary hopeless irreligion, that condition of the whole race, so fearful yet so exactly described in the Apostle's words 'having no hope and without God in the world' — all this is a vision to dizzy and appal; and inflicts upon the mind the sense of a profound mystery, which is absolutely beyond human solution."

The Christian solves it by the light of revelation; he goes back to that moment when man first sinned against his Creator, and

> Earth felt the wound, and Nature from her seat
> Sighing through all her works gave signs of woe
> That all was lost.

As originally created, man was at one with God: he was possessed of supernatural life which is best described as a participation in the life of God Himself. In addition, our first parents enjoyed other gifts which had a wonderfully ennobling influence on them, making their bodies subject to reason, exempt from pain and death, and destined for immortality.

Theologians are not agreed as to the precise differences that must be recognized between sanctifying grace and those other gifts that went to complete the original justice of the first man and woman. But the important thing in this original state was the divine life of sanctifying grace. On that all are agreed. When Adam and Eve rebelled the important thing they lost was precisely this supernatural life of grace. The other gifts went as a matter of course, and their immediate loss was very evident and conspicuous. Reason was no longer as subservient as it had been to God; the body was no longer entirely subject to the spirit; pain and suffering became man's lot. But the real calamity was the privation of sanctifying grace which had made man the friend of God, and heir to the kingdom of heaven.

To what extent the nature of man was injured in its constitutive faculties by this Fall has given rise to many controversies. The Church has definitely excluded one solution, which held that man was essentially corrupt as a result: she does not accept the essential corruption of human nature and thus rejects any kind of radical pessimism. But in as much as the really vital thing in man's original estate, the gift of divine life, has been won back again by Jesus Christ the Church endorses a fundamental optimism which stakes its faith on the Cross of Christ and on Christ's subsequent Resurrection. "For if by one man's offense death reigned through one; much more they who receive abundance of grace, and of the gift, and of justice, shall reign in life through One, Jesus Christ. Therefore as by the offense of one, unto all men condemnation; so also by the justice of One, unto all men to justification of life."[2] This optimism of the Church is an optimism which, knowing the facts of human life, believes in the power of God to realize human values finally and effectively. "For we preach Christ crucified, unto the Jews indeed a stumbling-block, and unto Gentiles, foolishness. But unto them that are called, both Jews and Greeks, Christ the power of God, and the wisdom of God."[3]

---

[2] Rom. 5:18–20.
[3] I Cor. 1:23–24.

# 13

# The Law of Life

The end and aim of all philosophy, remarked the pagan Plato, is to teach men how to die. Had he in mind merely a deathbed scene, which would mark the triumph of a life's philosophy, Plato scarcely grasped the fullest meaning of his dictum. He who awaits a final death wherein to practice his philosophy runs the risk of failure. But there is another death, a death in the midst of life, which guarantees the success of final death. That death in miniature is renunciation, and we may strengthen the phrase of Plato by saying that renunciation is the most striking lesson of all philosophy. According to the dictates of sane philosophy renunciation is the deepest law of all finite creaturehood. As such it is the very law of human life. In a word, renunciation is man's debt to God and to his own self.

It is interesting to remark the extent to which philosophy practices renunciation. Its final gesture, once it has come in sight of God, is one of self-abasement. That God exists, philosophy proclaims. That God is a personal God, philosophy is equally certain, but as to how and in what manner personality is realized in God, philosophy is mute. The final word of philosophy on God is that God in His Godhead infinitely transcends the powers of human reason. In that attitude philosophy pays its God the homage of its silence.

Philosophy proves that renunciation is the creature's debt to God. Interested in a final and convincing view of things, it tends more and more to see reality in a divine perspective: it is essentially theocentric. Not the least of philosophy's educational advantages is that it helps a man to get beyond the solid stability of his physical universe and to discount in the light of God's greater Reality the relief of the world around him. Spontaneously men are inclined to take short views of things and to round off the finite world as a kind of absolute in miniature. For the philosopher the universe in itself is dark and full of mystery as long as reason is content to grope within its narrow confines; only when his mind begins to view it in the light of God is he satisfied that somewhere at least all is clear and intelligible. By then the universe begins to lose some of its obtrusiveness for the senses, it falls into the background and God stands forth as Creative Source, Constant Upholder, and Supreme Good. Were God not, nothing could be; He unknown, the universe is but a half-truth akin to error.

If creation is at all intelligible, endowed with meaning, it is because of God. As Source of being, and being is the common denominator of all creation, God is the Source of all that can boast a right to being, of all that is and is not yet, of all that makes for life and progress in the universe entire. This is the only perspective in which philosophy can find content. And as a debt to God renunciation demands that the human mind in quest of ultimate viewpoints cannot rest until it begins to view the world itself in this divine perspective.

The instrument of philosophic inquiry is intelligence. But intelligence has a role to play in the life of man. It is the light which guides the path of life and its vision must be the inspiration of the art of living. For if intelligence indicates that God is the only Absolute in the realm of speculation, it is for man in his practical life to retain this same vision clear and compelling as the guide of life. For if the natural journey for the human mind is out beyond creation to God, this must also be the path followed by man's deep affections. The *itinerarium "mentis" ad Deum* must become an *itineratio "cordis."* Just as in its effort to discover ultimate explanations the human mind must renounce the finite world, so in its effort to discover ultimates for its action the human will cannot rest satisfied with any finite object in and for itself exclusively. Renunciation, then, is man's debt to God.

This fundamental relation of the universe as a whole to God carries with it that interrelation of parts which is the basis of unity and order in the world. To speak of order is to imply hierarchy and subordination of part to whole: sacrifice in favor of harmony is of the very essence of reality. It is just the paradox of this sacrifice and renunciation that it is a condition of all true harmony and order in the universe. The same paradox holds true in man's renunciation. To renounce the finite is ultimately to "gain" it in its ultimate truth and goodness and beauty. The mind which renounces the finite as self-explanatory enriches itself with the truth of God; the heart which renounces the finite as completely satisfying is enriched by the possession of God and escapes the snare of giving finite objects the delusion of infinite attractiveness; the spirit which looks beyond created beauty to its Primal Source is rewarded with the vision of God. To discover God in this way is to find the world for what it really is, a participation in God's truth and goodness and beauty.

Renunciation, philosophy teaches, is also man's debt to self. If personality is the chief value in the universe, and all philosophy teaches that man's fundamental duty is self-perfection and development, how can it be said that renunciation is man's debt to self? It is quite true that man's proximate end in life is the conservation and development of his personality with due regard to the same right and duty in other persons. The proof of this is that every finite nature tends to its proper good as to its end, and the human person is a finite being with characteristic tendencies and a perfection in harmony with its nature. The human person is an individual substance endowed with rational nature and subsisting in itself. Hence its perfection is brought about if man's rational nature is perfected and if his character of subsistence is enhanced. But how is man's rational nature to be developed if not by a renunciation of the lower elements in his life? In every man there are two levels of life, the biological life he shares with animals, and the spiritual life that is his as man. The biological life within him has certain tendencies. And every instinct in him is good. But does that mean that man's every instinct must have full play and be allowed unimpeded growth? Obviously not. These instincts seek their own particular goods and for each to have free rein would be to lead chaos and anarchy in his life. What must predominate in man is evidently the good of man as man. Man is man by reason. Hence man can be fully human only in so far as he renounces certain forms of development for what is truly human development. This necessary subordination of the lower instinctive life to the ends of mind is not destruction, not a stunting of human growth, but the only development open to him as man; that is, as being endowed with reason.

In this renunciation only is it possible for man to achieve his freedom as a human person. Man's freedom realizes itself by an increasing independence of his lower appetites, and he is really free only in so far as his reason can dominate his senses and allow him to follow what is best and noblest. This freedom is a necessary condition for any kind of real perfection in life.

This renunciation must make its way into the very heart of the human self, for if life is troubled by movements of sensible appetites there are also deviations that have their origin in man's own spirit, deviations that come from pride and vanity and self-love. But if we are clearly to see into this deeper aspect of the problem we must ask ourselves in what precisely does self-perfection for the finite person consist. The only answer possible is that self's greatest debt to self is again renunciation.

The philosophic reason for this statement is that no finite self has within wherewith to satisfy its hunger for life. Man's deepest urge is dictated by the needs of intellect and will, needs that point to God as the Supreme Good. Hence, no matter what natural perfection may reside in any finite nature, be it man or angel, the finite self can never be unto itself its ultimate end or goal. The object for which the finite nature craves is not something within itself, but outside, beyond it — God. But if it is deeply written in their natures that for perfection they must look to God, it follows that in their free and conscious activity both man and angel must elect for God. But to elect for God as their Supreme Good and Final End is to renounce self, not as a principle of activity, but as the goal and ultimate end of life. The finite intellectual creature, then, no matter of what order, may not seek itself exclusively or concentrate within itself for all the perfection of which it is capable. In the event of God's stooping down to elevate a finite intellectual nature to an end beyond its powers, the creature must be ready to die to self, to renounce that natural perfection which it might attain by its own natural activity, to attain a greater Self of which, by the aid of God, it is capable.

Viewed in the light of such considerations we see the full significance of the Fall of the Angels with which we are familiar from the Scripture. The sin of the angels was really a refusal on their part to accept the law of renunciation: they preferred to inhere in the natural perfection of their own selfhood than to accept a supernatural destiny which would mean the foregoing of their natural self in favor of the supernatural Self offered to them by God. In desiring to be like to God they thought to find in the contemplation of their own essence that perfect felicity which, by right of nature, belongs to God alone. In doing this, the fallen angels simply missed a form of higher self-realization which would have been possible, by God's aid, had they renounced self as their ultimate end to subordinate themselves to the really ultimate End of everything — God.

The creature is bound to seek the ultimate end. Not

to do so is to make self the end and goal of life. For man to fix for himself a goal of life, a *ne plus ultra,* is to fall into a similar error. No matter what measure of self-realization is possible, a natural beatitude for human life can never destroy the finite being's inherent tendency toward the really final end which is not a part of nature, but nature's End. But if the human self is not the ultimate end of life, it must renounce its pretension to set a limit to life's possible perfection. The ultimate duty of every finite self to self is that of renunciation.

We cannot view the modern rejection of the supernatural without going back in thought to that moment when proud created intelligence refused to die to self that it might possess a life divine of which it was infinitely unworthy. And this rejection has its roots in an egoism that is deep and metaphysical. Modern philosophy is centered in man, not in God. From Descartes to Fichte, passing through Kant, man becomes increasingly central. If we look at modern religious thought as divorced from Christian philosophy, a similar conclusion is forced upon us. "The Reformation," writes M. J. Maritain, "unbridled the human self in the spiritual and religious order as the Renaissance (I mean the secret spirit of the Renaissance) unbridled the human self in the order of natural and sensible activities."

But if human personality is to realize itself, that realization can only come from self-development in its true order. Personality is the most perfect thing on earth; but its perfection lies in its essential subordination to God alone. Personality is not to be confounded with individuality merely, for while personality applies only to complete individual substances of the rational nature, individuality is common to man and beast. "To develop one's individuality is to live the egotistical life of the passions, to make oneself the center of everything, and end finally by being the slave of a thousand passing goods which bring us a wretched momentary joy. Personality, on the contrary, increases as the soul rises above the sensible world and by intelligence and will binds itself more closely to what makes the life of the spirit. The philosophers have caught sight of it, but the saints especially have understood that the full development of our poor personality consists in losing it in some way in that of God, who alone possesses personality in the perfect sense of the word, for He alone is absolutely independent in His being and action."[1]

This is brought about by foregoing self as the goal of life, but as a principle of action the human self remains with all that it implies by way of natural temperament, particular circumstances, and other individuating characteristics. Just as in assuming human nature God did not wish to absorb or destroy it, so the Spirit of Christ in the lives of Christians does not annihilate temperament or character. Sanctity is genius in holiness, and if there is but one essential holiness in the world, there are and can be as many expressions of it in life as there are individuals. The worth of life lies in being one with God in Christ; the glory of life is the diversity in unity which this wedding of humanity and divinity has given to the world.

---

[1]Garrigou-Lagrange, O.P., R., *Le sens commun*, pp. 332–33.